"I have known Jessica since her Crown College days. It was heart-wrenching to read of her emotional and spiritual struggles in dealing with the death of her son Ethan and her journey of learning to trust God in all things. She believes that God can use her journey to minister to others, as she states so well in her book: '...this is where I will serve—along this dark road that has only been traveled by a few, and can only be understood by someone who has walked the path herself'."

Gary Benedict, President,
The U.S. Christian and
Missionary Alliance

Do You Trust Me?

Allowing Hope to Triumph Over Tragedy

Jessica Leigh Johnson

WestBow
PRESS
A DIVISION OF THOMAS NELSON

WestBow Press books may be ordered through booksellers or by contacting:

WestBow Press
A Division of Thomas Nelson
1663 Liberty Drive
Bloomington, IN 47403
www.westbowpress.com
1-(866) 928-1240

Because of the dynamic nature of the Internet, any web addresses or links contained in this book may have changed since publication and may no longer be valid. The views expressed in this work are solely those of the author and do not necessarily reflect the views of the publisher, and the publisher hereby disclaims any responsibility for them.

Any people depicted in stock imagery provided by Thinkstock are models, and such images are being used for illustrative purposes only.
Certain stock imagery © Thinkstock.

Cover photography by Jessica L. Johnson

ISBN: 978-1-4497-5068-8 (sc)
ISBN: 978-1-4497-5069-5 (hc)
ISBN: 978-1-4497-5067-1 (e)

Library of Congress Control Number: 2012908049

Printed in the United States of America

WestBow Press rev. date:05/11/2012

To Ethan. During your short life you touched so many. Now may the story of your life continue to offer hope to those who are hurting. I will always be proud of you for enduring all that was asked of you and look forward to seeing you in heaven...hopefully soon! I miss those big baby blues. I love you so much.

"Praise be to the God and Father of our Lord Jesus Christ, the Father of compassion and the God of all comfort, who comforts us in all our troubles, so that we can comfort those in any trouble with the comfort we ourselves have received from God."

2 Corinthians 1:3–4

Contents

Preface

There are times in our lives that our faith—everything we believe to be true—is shaken to the very core. For me, that time came when my son became very ill and suddenly passed away. The days and months that followed were the hardest of my life. The death of my child called into question everything that I took for granted as truth—everything I thought I understood about God. For the first time in my life, I was no longer sure that God heard my prayers, or that he even cared about me anymore. I began to doubt whether or not I could trust him with the things most precious to me: my children.

The idea of writing a book about my experience with the loss of my child has been lingering in the back of my mind for some time, but the timing was never right. I hadn't yet reached the point where I felt at peace with what had happened in my life. If I had written my family's story within the first five years after losing our son, the book would have had one serious flaw: it wouldn't have had an ending. Or if it did, it would have been one heck of a cliff-hanger! I could probably have summed up the entire story in a few sentences: "I lost my little boy even though I prayed that he would be healed. I still don't really understand what happened, and now I can't trust God with anything." The end. I probably would have entitled it, *What Was That All About?* Sound like a must-read? I didn't think so. It has only been recently that I truly feel I have come to the end of my story, or at least this chapter of it. Finally, after five years, I feel that I have reached a place of resolution to the conflict which losing my son had created in my life—a conflict of faith and trust.

Another reason that I have chosen to write about my personal struggles with grief and trusting God is the simple fact that when I was going through the early days following my son's death, a book like this would have been really helpful. I remember feeling as though I were the only person in the world who had ever experienced something as tragic as the loss of a child. Well-meaning friends and acquaintances would come up to my husband and me and tell us that they knew exactly how we felt because they had lost their grandfather several years earlier—or their dog. Needless to say, it's just not the same thing.

My hope is that someone out there will read this and find some comfort—some glimmer of hope that yes, in fact, things will get better…eventually. And as hard as it may be to believe during the darkest of days, we *can* trust God, even if it seems he has let us down in the biggest possible way. It is for this reason that I share my family's story.

Introduction

As much as I would like to believe that I am still twenty-five, I have to admit that I am getting...*older*. Just the other day I said to my husband, "Life is going by so fast!" Only *old* people are supposed to say things like that. It's like I just blinked, and suddenly my firstborn is heading to middle school, my five-year-old has already lost his first tooth, and my baby is potty trained. *Seriously? No more diapers? Why does that make me sad?*

I don't like it when people look at my children and say, "My, they're getting so big." It just makes me cringe. *You take that back!* Wasn't it just yesterday that they were little babies? Is it really okay to finally take those plastic protectors out of all the electrical outlets? I think I'll just leave them there a little while longer. They make me happy.

With life passing by at lightning speed, it is no surprise that I cannot remember many of the moments that I have lived. I can't remember what I did for my fourth birthday, or who came to my party—if I even had a party. I don't have a clue how I felt on my first day of school. Knowing me I probably cried, but that's only a guess because the memory of what should have been a monumental moment has been neatly tucked away in some far-off mental storage space in my brain. It is possible that several years down the road, a familiar smell or a certain song might trigger some of these long-forgotten memories, but it will only be a matter of time before they fade away again.

Among all of the moments that have made up my life so far, there are a select few that I remember vividly. They cannot be forgotten. These are moments that were truly life-changing. In these moments, time seemed to stand still. Even as they were happening, I knew that once these moments passed, my life would never be the same.

The first of these moments took place during the early morning hours of July 5, 1984—a month before my seventh birthday. Sometime in the middle of the night, I was awakened by loud noises coming from my parents' bedroom. I got out of my bed, opened my bedroom door, and peered into the next room only to see my dad thrashing uncontrollably on the bed. My mom was standing there, leaning over him, frantically trying to help him, but I could tell she didn't know what to do.

"Jessica, go back to your room!" my mom shouted. I stood there for a moment, almost frozen, staring at my dad before eventually running back into my room. My mom had never yelled at me before. I had never been so scared. I closed my bedroom door and waited for my mom to come and tell me what was going on. Even though I wasn't quite seven years old, I knew something was really wrong with my dad.

Several minutes later, my grandparents arrived, and I was ushered into the spare bedroom to wait with them. Nobody said a word as an ambulance arrived, and paramedics walked up the stairs and lifted my dad onto a gurney. I watched out the second-story window as my dad was loaded into the back of the waiting ambulance and eventually taken to the hospital. I may have been young, but I was old enough to know that after that moment, my life would never be the same.

The second time-stopping moment occurred on March 8, 1998. It was the moment when I first saw my husband, Bart, although at the time I never would have dreamed I would actually marry him someday. I was a junior in college, and I was leading a youth group meeting in the basement of the small church where I worked. In the middle of a small-group activity, he just appeared at the door. From that moment on, I was sure of one thing: if I didn't marry him, I would never be satisfied with anyone else.

I may not remember the topic of conversation that night at youth group, or which kids had shown up, but that moment—the way time actually seemed to stop when he walked through that door and I saw him for the first time—will never be forgotten as long as I live. Meeting Bart changed my life forever.

There is one other moment, which, as painful as it was, will be forever etched into my memory. It was late at night on April 2, 2006. My husband and I were standing together in the pediatric intensive care unit of the University of Minnesota Medical Center in Minneapolis. Our infant son was lying in a bed in the corner of the room, and one of the doctors pulled us aside to speak privately.

"Do you remember what you asked me earlier?" she began. "To let you know when there was nothing more we could do?"

"Yes," I replied.

"Well, it's that time."

Those are words that I will never forget. Once those words were out of the doctor's mouth, there was no going back. The course of my life was completely altered. Before the doctor spoke those words, there was still a chance that our son would survive. We still had three children and could still hold out hope that someday soon we could all go home and forget the nightmare that we had been living for the two weeks leading up to that moment. But once the words were spoken, everything changed. It was a turning point not only in the way I lived my life, in my day-to-day existence, but also in my spiritual life.

From that moment until today, whenever I am faced with a crisis—whenever I have to make the decision whether to trust God or not—it is as if God himself is standing right in front of me. He has his hands on my shoulders, begging for my undivided attention, and he is asking me, "Do you trust me?"

Before I can answer, I can only stand still while the video montage of life-changing moments—both good and bad—plays over and over again in my mind like a highlight film of my past, and all I can give him for an answer is: *I don't know if I can.*

1

Beginnings

I loved being a kid. Up until I was about seven years old, my childhood would have been considered typical of any kid who grew up during the eighties. I woke up every Saturday morning in time to watch *Smurfs*, and then spent the rest of the day playing with Barbies and LEGOs, or rescuing orphaned babies from the Cabbage Patch. I listened to Michael Jackson, Billy Joel, and Madonna on my record player, and my all-time favorite movie was *The Wizard of Oz*.

I grew up as an only child in Stow, Ohio—the same town in which my dad grew up. My family moved into a nice house in a nice neighborhood when I was three years old, and I lived in the same house until the day I left for college. My mother was a third grade teacher and my dad worked in transportation management; although he had been unemployed for almost a year before he finally landed a job ordering and tracking shipments for a design firm in Akron, Ohio. He had been working for this firm for only two months, and all the while he had been suffering from terrible headaches. The doctors chalked it up to the stress of working with a bunch of women all day long.

Then in the early hours of July 5, 1984, about a month before my seventh birthday, everything in my world was altered in a matter of seconds. After suffering from another severe headache, my dad returned home early from a Fourth of July picnic and went straight to bed. Around 2:00 a.m., he suffered a grand mal seizure. My mom called the ambulance and ordered me to stay in my room.

My dad was diagnosed with stage-two malignant glioma: a cancerous brain tumor. The doctors supposed that the tumor had been slowly growing for most of my dad's life, finally making its presence known with those terrible headaches he had been having. My dad had surgery to remove the tumor the next day, although the surgeons could not get all of it. The post-surgery prognosis was not good. His doctors figured he would live two more years at the most.

The surgery left my dad paralyzed on the left side, from the neck down. Several weeks after the surgery, when he finally returned home from the hospital, my dad was able to walk with a cane. Eventually, his condition worsened, and he became bedridden. My dad was over six feet tall, and my mom, being only five-foot-two, could not help him up the stairs to sleep in their bedroom anymore. It was even becoming difficult for her to help him get to the bathroom, or to the kitchen for meals, so he spent most of his time lying in a hospital bed in our living room.

While my mom was at work and I was at school, someone had to stay at our house with my dad because he could not be left alone. My two sets of grandparents would stay with him one or two days each, and on the other days volunteers from several churches would stay. Occasionally there would be scheduling conflicts, so visiting nurses would have to come to our house. On these days, I would get off the bus after school, walk into my house, and not even know the person who greeted me at the door. These were the days that I simply went straight up to my room; it was better than having an awkward conversation with a complete stranger. Unfortunately, this caused me to miss out on spending time with my dad—time that was running out, although I didn't know it then.

I was aware that my dad had a brain tumor; that was made clear from the beginning. What I didn't know was that it was cancer, and he was dying from it. No one mentioned that to me, probably to protect me. I thought my dad would be around forever, sitting in his wheelchair or lying in his hospital bed. I even pictured myself pushing his wheelchair down the aisle at my wedding.

Although my dad lived more than twice as long as the doctors predicted, the cancer eventually won out. On December 8, 1988, I was walking home from the bus stop after a typical day in sixth grade when I noticed that my grandparents' car was in the driveway, along with my mother's car. My mom didn't usually arrive home until an hour after I got off the bus, so I knew that something was wrong.

When I got inside, my grandma greeted me. One look into the family room told me that my dad was not in his hospital bed.

"What happened to Daddy?" I asked.

My grandma looked at my mom, and then back at me. "Why don't you go upstairs with your mom," she said. "She'll tell you everything."

When I arrived upstairs, my mom took me into her room, sat me on her bed, and told me that my dad had passed away. She explained that my grandparents just couldn't get him to wake up that morning. They called my mom at work, and an ambulance came to take my dad to the hospital. There my mom and grandparents were told that my dad had actually slipped into a coma. He passed away later that day. I never got a chance to say goodbye.

After that it was just my mom and me, and that was fine—at least, it was fine with me. A little over a year after my dad passed away, my mom started dating her high school sweetheart. They eventually got engaged, and then got married in June of 1990, the summer before my eighth grade year. It would be an understatement to say that I did not handle this well. First of all, I was happy with the way things were—just my mom and me. Combine that with the fact that I was thirteen years old, and you have a recipe for disaster. I don't need to go into detail; I'll just say that things got off to a rather rocky start.

2

Trusting God with the
Little Things

Before my dad got sick, my parents and I attended church once in a while. When I was a child, God was someone that I believed in, but I didn't really know him. I had no relationship with him whatsoever. Whenever I would think about God, the images in my mind would be accompanied by loud claps of thunder and flashes of lightning. God was definitely someone to be feared, but not necessarily someone to love. To me, he was more of a distant, cosmic overseer who looked down on us from time to time, but I didn't think he had any real interest or involvement in the lives of us lowly humans.

When my mother got married again, she and my new stepfather began attending a different church—not the one I went to when I was younger—and they made me go with them every Sunday. This was an unwelcomed lifestyle change for me, since I had gotten used to sleeping in on Sundays. To me, Sunday was just another Saturday, except the cartoons weren't as good. We didn't go to church during the four and a half years that my father was sick; it was hard enough just to get to the grocery store. Now out of nowhere, we had become regular church attendees.

Every Sunday morning I reluctantly got up and went to church—not that I had much choice in the matter. I also started attending the junior high Sunday school class and went to youth group every Wednesday night (again, not my choice).

The youth pastor at my new church, Pastor Rudy, was one of the most energetic and excited people I had ever met. He jumped up and down when he preached, played the keyboard and sang worship songs with real passion, and was literally drenched in sweat by the end of each Wednesday night youth group meeting. Pastor Rudy made going to church fun, which was something I never thought possible. Of course I never admitted this to my stepdad; I was still mad at him for making me go against my will. It was in youth group that I learned that I could actually have a personal relationship with God, and that he had a plan for my life. Even though I had attended church as a young child, I had never heard any of this before.

By the start of eighth grade, I stopped fighting my stepdad about going to church and youth group, accepted the fact that he may have been *slightly* right, and gave my life to the Lord at a Sunday evening church service. I remember our senior pastor asking anyone who would like to receive Christ as his or her Lord and Savior to draw the sign of the cross with his or her foot on the carpet. I appreciated that method of commitment-making—no hand raising required, no long, embarrassing march up to the altar. No one but God and I would have to know.

Trusting God with my eternal destiny? *Check.* That was the biggie, right? Little did I know that the biggest thing I was to trust God with—my life—would be the easiest thing. I mean, who in her right mind would want to go to hell if given the choice? Trusting God would prove to be more difficult in the years to come.

Those next few years held many big decisions about the future: where to go to college, what major to choose, whom to marry. Surprisingly, each of these decisions came easily for me because in each situation I felt a clear sense of direction from God.

During my junior year of high school, the band from Crown College, a small Christian college in Minnesota, came to my church to give a concert during the evening service. Two recruiters from the college had set up a table in the foyer with pamphlets and brochures about the school for people to pick up and take home with them. My stepdad *forced* me to take a course catalog home with me, even though I had already decided where I was going to college. I planned on following most of my youth group friends to a small Christian college in New York. It was only seven hours from home—not fifteen like Crown College. I hadn't been away from home more than a few days at a time, and I had never been more than half an hour away from my mom in my entire life. There was no way I was going all the way to Minnesota. But to appease my stepdad, I took the catalog home (and tossed it in the back of my closet).

Over the course of that year, every time I would think about college I would have an uneasy feeling about going to New York. Even after visiting the school with some other students from my youth group, I felt absolutely no confirmation that I was supposed to go there. For some reason, Crown College kept coming to my mind—and it would not go away.

I threw you in the back of my closet, Crown College. Remember?

Well, I knew better than to ignore the Lord's promptings for too long, so eventually, I took that Crown catalog out of its hiding place, dusted it off, and looked through it. Something about the school really impressed me, and I finally had that peaceful feeling I was waiting for. So after very little prayer, I relied on an even *more* reliable decision-making tool—the strong gut feeling—and made the decision to go to Crown College after all. I sent in my application and was accepted—case closed. I had my entire future planned out before the start of my senior year of high school.

Still, for some reason, my parents insisted that we drive all the way to Minnesota to check out the school. They probably needed to see it for themselves, since they would be spending a small fortune on my tuition. Visiting the campus only further confirmed that I had made the right choice. As soon as our rented minivan turned onto the driveway and headed onto the Crown College campus, I was convinced that this was where the Lord was calling me; I could just feel it. And the accents of those Minnesotan students that I met while I was there—*so cute.* I even started to pronounce words with an over-exaggerated long *o*, so I would be sure to fit in.

I spent my first two years at Crown bouncing from one department to another, unsure about what I should choose for a major. Because I believed I had been called into full-time ministry, I started out in the world missions department. After a year of missions classes, I realized that being a missionary was not what God had planned for me. So after my freshman year, I changed my major to history. One night toward the end of my sophomore year, as I lay in bed in my dorm room, I looked over the course offerings in the latest Crown catalog. The catalog had served me well in the past; maybe it would come through again.

After browsing through the entire catalog, I discovered that the Christian education major offered the two things I wanted most: the most fun classes and the professors I loved. But with everything that was so seemingly perfect about this educational track, there was one little catch: the Christian education degree could not be completed without fulfilling the dreaded six-month internship. That would mean six months away from my safe, sheltered existence at Crown College. I would have to spend six months away from all of my friends. Three of those months would be during the summer, which meant one entire summer of not going home to Ohio. How would I ever tell my mother?

I decided to run away from the Lord—for a little while. I changed my major to Bible and theology. I stayed with that for about three months. But somehow, when I started my junior year, I found myself in the youth ministries/Christian education department. Even though it may have taken me a little while to come around, I knew that it was better to be in the Lord's will than outside of it, even if it scared the living daylights out of me. It didn't take long to once again feel that following the Lord's leading would lead to abundant blessings. The first event that the youth ministries/Christian education department held to kick off the fall of 1997 was a yacht cruise around beautiful Lake Minnetonka, just outside of Minneapolis. Yes, I had definitely chosen the right major.

After my first semester in the Christian education program, the internship lurked ever nearer. By the start of the spring semester in January 1998, it was getting harder and harder to push it to the back of my mind. I had spent that fall pretending it wasn't going to happen. Maybe things would change, and the internship would no longer be a requirement, but rather an *option*. No such luck. By this time I had a boyfriend, and my best friend was engaged. I was leaving at the end of a twelve-week block of classes, and I would miss everything! I would return from the internship in time to begin my senior year after all of my friends had graduated.

At first, I was told that my internship would take place in Rockville, Maryland. That was way too far away from Crown. How would I ever make it back to see my friends? The word *internship* had taken on a very negative connotation—so much so that my friends and I decided we would not even speak of it. We just pretended that it wasn't going to happen.

By the time the last students in the youth ministries/Christian education department were being given their internship assignments, mine suddenly fell through. Due to of a lack of funding, the church in Maryland could not host a youth intern. Because of this, I began doubting whether or not I had made a mistake when I chose the Christian education major. Maybe I had misinterpreted God's leading, and he had never intended for me to work in ministry at all.

Fortunately, a few days later, the professor in charge of the internship placements received a phone call from the pastor of a small church in northern Minnesota. The pastor explained that the intern who was supposed to come to his church had backed out. The pastor and his church were still interested in hosting an intern, so I got the job.

In late February, after a much-dreaded departure from Crown College, I drove three and a half hours north to this small town in the north woods of Minnesota. I would spend the next six months being a youth pastor to a group of about thirty kids combined from two separate, smaller churches. I would split my Sundays between the two churches, and the youth group would meet as one combined group on Wednesday nights.

After church on my first Sunday as an official intern youth pastor, I was invited out to lunch by a nice family named the Johnson family. Mr. and Mrs. Johnson, along with four of their five children—two of whom were in the youth group—took me out to McDonald's. They also invited me over to their house that Thursday night for supper. After that first evening with them, I ended up spending every Thursday evening at the Johnsons' house. Since two of their children were in the youth group, I considered my time at their house to be *ministry*.

In addition to the two kids in youth group, the Johnsons also had one daughter in college and one who was in fifth grade. And then there was their oldest son, the infamous Bart, who was away at college—but not to worry—I heard plenty about him, whether I wanted to or not. "*Bart* spent the spring of '97 sandbagging in Fargo when the Red River flooded. *Bart* plays football at Moorhead State University. *Bart* gets straight A's. *Bart* got this scholarship, and that scholarship and this scholarship..." I think I've made my point. Seriously, who were they trying to fool? No one's *that* perfect. I figured these parents must be seriously disillusioned. Their son played college football at a *state* school. Hello? I knew all about what went on among state college football players—or at least I thought I did.

That brings me to March 8, 1998, and one of those unforgettable moments. It was a Wednesday night, and I was in the church basement leading youth group. The kids were working on a project in small groups, and I was walking from one group to another when a very tall, handsome man walked into the room. He was so handsome, in fact, that I suddenly forgot that I had a boyfriend back at Crown. I watched him as he talked to one of the adult youth workers, Nolan, who was in his mid-thirties. I assumed this guy was also in his thirties; he looked older. I figured the two of them must be coworkers at the mill, or maybe they were friends. Nolan and his wife called me over to meet this stranger, and I could *not* look him in the eyes. Instead I just stared at the floor—I was in awe. Nolan said, "Jessica, this is Bart Johnson, the Johnsons' oldest son."

What? The sand-bagging, straight-A-getting, state college football player? What is he doing at youth group? I came to find out I was very wrong to make generalizations about *all* state college football players. There was at least one out there who was just as virtuous and full of integrity as his parents believed him to be. I would also find out later that Bart had only come to youth group that night because his dad told him he should check out the new youth leader, and that is something for which I will be forever grateful.

That night I could not fall asleep. I knew that something had changed. Even though I had a boyfriend, I had just met the man who would from then on be the standard by which all current and future boyfriends would be measured. Fortunately for me, there were no future boyfriends, besides Bart. He and I started dating that June.

The remaining two months of my internship went well—and quickly. I had learned that I could do things that scared me, as long as the Lord was leading me. After all, he was the one doing the hard stuff. I was simply his hands and feet. By December, Bart and I were engaged. God had definitely scored a touchdown this time. He had picked the perfect person for me to marry, and I knew there was no way I could have found him on my own. It was only because I had followed God—kicking and screaming all the way—to northern Minnesota.

By this time I had grown pretty accustomed to a certain pattern in my life: the Holy Spirit would impress upon my heart what I was supposed to do, and I would do it. Once I allowed God to be the Lord of my life, everything seemed to work out better than I could have imagined—definitely better than if I would have planned things out myself. Trusting God was easy because he was proving himself to be trustworthy again and again.

3

The Midas Touch

I have always tended to be a worrier, while Bart had this philosophy of life: *Go with the flow.* He was confident that any minor obstacles in life could be overcome eventually, so there was never any need to worry. Everything always seemed to work out for Bart, and since I married him, things began to work out well for me, also. I had been grafted into his family's legacy of spiritual blessings. Now I, too, would be successful in every endeavor. This was definitely a far cry from my usual glass-half-empty approach to life. It seemed to me that everything Bart touched turned to gold. He accomplished everything he ever set out to do.

Bart and I spent our first year of married life in Fargo, North Dakota, while Bart finished up his degree in mechanical engineering at NDSU. After graduating from college, Bart decided to attend graduate school at the University of Michigan, so we moved to Ann Arbor. While Bart was in grad school, I worked at the university as a secretary for the engineering department. In October, two months after we arrived in Ann Arbor, I found out I was pregnant with our first child. I was supposed to be excited. This was what I had wanted for several months, but when I saw that little purple line on the pregnancy test I was scared to death. I didn't know how to be pregnant! How was I supposed to keep a baby that I couldn't even see alive for nine months? Wasn't there something special I was supposed to be doing? Wasn't there some kind of cheese I was supposed to avoid eating? The nurse at the clinic told me that I couldn't even get an appointment with a doctor until I was twelve weeks along. What if I made some kind of horrible mistake before then?

The other thing that worried me was the timing of it all. Bart graduated in late April, and the baby was due in the end of May. According to our rental agreement with married student housing, we had to be out of our apartment by the end of June. What were we supposed to do if the baby was late? What if the baby was born after our student insurance expired and we had to pay for the whole birth with our own money?

Bart had accepted a job as a mechanical engineer at John Deere in Dubuque, Iowa that would start the last week of June. I wondered what would happen if I hadn't had the baby by the time we moved, and I went into labor in a U-Haul truck in the middle of the highway somewhere between Michigan and Iowa. I never ran out of things to worry about.

By this time, I was quickly discovering that being a Christian and being married was much more difficult than being a single Christian. Things were so much more complicated now that I was part of a couple. Once Bart was added to the equation, a lot of things in my life depended upon him and what he wanted to do. Gone were the days of God telling me what to do and me doing it. Now it was God telling Bart what to do, and Bart telling me what God wanted him to do, and me agreeing with it—or not. If I didn't agree, Bart would ask me to pray about it until I did agree, and usually, I would end up seeing things his way.

Looking back, I can see that this was the beginning of a growing distance between me and God. I began to feel disconnected from him. It seemed like God wasn't speaking directly to me anymore. He wasn't leading me in any certain direction whatsoever. He was now speaking to Bart, leading Bart, and I was simply expected to follow. I no longer felt like God had a unique and special plan for me as an individual, and I didn't exactly know how to deal with that. When I first became a Christian, the one thing I found most appealing was the fact that God had a plan for my life. Once I got married, though, I began to see less and less evidence to support that claim. It was disappointing, to say the least.

In late April, Bart graduated from the University of Michigan with his Masters of Science in Engineering, although he still had some work to do to finish up the industry project that went along with the degree. I, of course, was still pregnant. When my due date came and went, with no sign of a baby, I started to feel depressed and anxious. We were moving in three weeks. I still had to pack up all of our belongings and get ready to move to Iowa. How was I supposed to do that with a brand new baby?

Whenever I talked to my grandmother about my due date, she would say she was praying that the baby would be born on my dad's birthday, which was in June. I told her that was cruel. I would have to be two weeks overdue to have a baby on my dad's birthday. Fortunately for my grandma, her prayers must not have fallen on deaf ears, because at 3:30 p.m. on my dad's birthday—two weeks after my due date—our daughter Emma was born. Two weeks after that, we packed all of our belongings into a U-Haul truck and headed to Iowa, with Emma strapped in an infant car seat between us. Those last few months in Ann Arbor were indeed stressful for me, but all of my worry was in vain because everything worked out just fine, just as Bart said it would.

When we arrived in Dubuque, we moved into our brand new house, and I began my new job as a stay-at-home mom. Bart started his job as a mechanical engineer at John Deere Dubuque Works designing backhoes. The world of academia was finally behind us, and I felt as though real life was just beginning.

When Emma was almost two years old, we had our second child. Baby Andrew was born on Bart's grandfather's birthday, which was also two weeks after my due date. Another baby born on someone else's birthday! Now we had a boy and a girl—a picture perfect family. We were indeed blessed. Bart was doing well at John Deere and was on the management track. This was good for him because it gave him the opportunity to earn more money and advance in his career. But it also meant that the company would move him to different facilities in different cities every three years or so, in order to expand his work experience. When we thought about how constantly moving would affect our family life, we weren't too excited. Also, after only a few years living in Iowa, Bart was becoming increasingly restless. He was used to living in northern Minnesota; he loved the woods and the great outdoors. He missed deer hunting in the fall with the men in his family. Summers usually spent at the family lake cabin were now spent in humid ninety-degree weather staring out the back window at a never-ending corn field. My idea of Iowa as the perfect location for our family—halfway between Bart's parents and my parents—was actually quite the opposite. Instead of seeing both families equally as often, we ended up not seeing either side, ever. At least that's how it felt; eight hours was still a long drive.

After three years with John Deere, Bart started to get ideas about making a career change. He had been an advisor to several college co-op students at John Deere, and had really enjoyed working with them. He wondered if he might enjoy teaching engineering at the community college level. He had come from a family of teachers, so maybe teaching was in his blood. And if nothing else, he would have his summers off!

One day, Bart went on the internet and looked up the job listings on the website of his hometown newspaper. He was pleasantly surprised to discover that there was an opening for a chemistry instructor at the community college. He asked me what I thought. Should he pursue this? He lovingly reminded me that when we first started dating, he had made it perfectly clear that he intended to move back home eventually, even though that was sixteen hours away from my home and my family. When he first asked me, I said that I would be happy to live in northern Minnesota. I don't think he would have married me if I would have said, "That's too far away." So obviously, I didn't say that. But now things had changed; we had two kids—my mother's only two grandchildren—and we would be taking them further away from her.

Just like every other time that I tried to run away from the Lord's will, I soon came to my senses. My past experience had taught me that I did not want to go against what the Lord wanted in my life, which had now become *Bart's* and my life. If this job opportunity was from God, then it would all work out. It would be better to be sixteen hours away from my family and *in* the Lord's will, than eight hours away and *not* in the Lord's will. I told Bart it was okay with me if he applied for the job. What could it hurt? He had no teaching experience. How was he qualified for this job? It was a long-shot at best, but deep in my heart I felt that he would get it. My husband could do anything he put his mind to.

After two interviews at the community college, Bart was offered the job as chemistry instructor. He gave his notice at John Deere, and we packed up our little family and drove eight hours north to Minnesota. We were fortunate enough to find a house to rent that would be available fifteen days before we needed to move in. This was just further proof that everything would always work out in the end if we simply trusted the Lord.

4

Everywhere, Red Flags

Our kids have always loved the Little Golden Book *Tootle*, about the little engine that liked to jump off the tracks and roll around in the meadow and make daisy chains. In this book, we learn that good engines *never* leave the tracks and *always* stop for a red flag waving.[1] When it came to our little son Andrew, there were plenty of red flags waving, but for some reason, we never stopped long enough to realize that we were heading into very dangerous territory.

Before our move back to Minnesota, when Andrew—whom I finally allowed to be called Andy after his first birthday—was four months old, he developed his first illness. This was strange to me because Emma hadn't gotten sick until she was about thirteen months old and had come down with Roseola. Even stranger to me was the fact that I was nursing Andy, which was supposed to help him fight off infections until his own immune system was strong enough to take over. Nevertheless, four-month-old Andrew had gotten a bad virus and had a very high fever.

He was so congested that he couldn't breathe through his nose at all, which was a problem since his only way of eating was by nursing; he needed to be able to breathe through his nose. Every time he was able to get a little milk into his stomach, the thick mucus that had built up in his lungs from the virus made him cough so hard that he would eventually throw up everything he had just eaten. As a result of this, our eighteen-pound, four-ounce four-month-old *grew* to be a sixteen-pound, eleven-ounce six-month-old. The virus took forever to "run its course," as the doctor said it would. The doctor even ordered blood tests, just to be sure he wasn't missing something (and yet somehow, he still was).

The blood test results showed that Andy's monocyte levels were elevated, although there was no presence of the Epstein-Barr virus that causes Mono. The best name the doctor could come up with to describe what Andy was fighting was a "Mono-like virus." The doctor had even said on more than one occasion that if Andy continued to lose weight, he would have to be hospitalized. Fortunately, that never happened.

Andy got his first ear infection at the age of eight months. Emma, who was two and a half years old at that time, had not had any. We figured Andy must take after his dad, who had suffered from frequent ear infections as a child; and Emma took after me, who had never had one. In every situation that presented itself, there was always some rational explanation for what was going on.

By the time we moved to Minnesota, Andy had been sick with *something* almost every month of his life. After one infection would clear, another one would begin. He had already had several ear infections, so by the time he was fifteen months old, the doctor was talking about putting tubes in Andy's ears. Even so, I was still comfortable with everything that was happening to Andy thus far. But the week that we moved into our little rental house in Minnesota, something happened that should have sent red flags waving all over the place.

It was only our second day in our new home. Unpacked boxes were lying all over the floor, and I can still remember sitting in our recliner with Andy, staring at the massive unpacking job that lay ahead of me. Andy had a cold, which was nothing new, but that day he spiked a fever of 102°. I remember he suddenly took in a very sharp breath and made a noise like a shout. Then his arms and legs twitched a few times, and he started to make weird noises, like he couldn't breathe and was sucking in air. His skin started to look blue. Then, as suddenly as it had started, he just fell asleep. I freaked! I didn't have a doctor yet in Minnesota, so I called my doctor back in Iowa who had been treating Andy for his other illnesses. The nurse there explained to me that it sounded like Andy had had a febrile seizure, and that I really should find a doctor in Minnesota and get Andy to the clinic.

After being asleep for a few minutes, Andy woke up and was very groggy. I did take him to see a pediatrician, and she set us up to have an EEG just to make sure that what Andy had was, indeed, a febrile seizure and not a symptom of something more serious like epilepsy or a brain tumor. I had had a febrile seizure when I was thirteen months old, and febrile seizures were known to run in families, so again, there was a rational explanation for Andy's seizure. But he ended up having another seizure that night and three more within the next four months.

The results of the EEG came back abnormal, which was probably due to the fact that I had held Andy while he slept through the procedure and my arm was putting pressure on one of the electrodes. Even so, the doctor ordered an MRI to make sure that truly was the case. Because our local hospital did not have an MRI unit at that time, we had to travel over an hour away to St. Mary's Hospital in Duluth, Minnesota to have the procedure done.

Andy was put under for the MRI, and while he was coming out of the anesthesia, he was placed in a bed. Because all of the beds in the regular children's ward were full, Andy was given a bed in the pediatric intensive care unit. As I sat next to his bed waiting for him to wake up, I had a very strange feeling—like this would not be the last time we would be in that intensive care unit in St. Mary's Hospital, and this was only a foreshadowing of something much worse which was to come. I tried to shake that nagging feeling, but that was easier said than done.

The MRI came back normal, causing us all to breathe a sigh of relief. Andy was only having febrile seizures—he did not have Epilepsy or a brain tumor. Still, the seizures concerned me. I had heard once that if a child had more than one febrile seizure in a year, then something more serious could be going on. Andy had five seizures in four months. The doctors were looking into the reasons why he was having so many seizures, and the answer was easy: because he was having so many high fevers. But they stopped their investigation there. It would have been very helpful if someone would have probed deeper into why he was having so many high fevers in the first place. That would have led the doctors to the reason for his constant infections and they would have solved the problem much sooner. Unfortunately, this did not occur.

Our new doctor said it was considered normal for a child to have up to twelve colds a year, and Andy was having twelve—one each month. So, we left it at that. Andy was on the high end of normal when it came to sickness. But was it still normal for a fifteen-month-old to have already had bronchitis twice, five ear infections, and five febrile seizures? In our limited understanding of all things medical, we simply trusted the doctors, whom we now understand are only human and do not know everything—just like us.

During one of Andy's many viral infections, I couldn't get him an appointment with our regular pediatrician so I took him to see a different doctor. Andy had been sick for several weeks and didn't seem to be getting better, and I wanted to see if there was any way the doctor could tell if he had something bacterial—something that could be treated with antibiotics. This doctor ordered a few blood tests and told us someone would call with the results.

The next day the doctor called back herself. I will never forget that conversation. She sounded very concerned.

"Andy's white cell count is quite high," she said. "We would expect to see that with a viral illness, but it's a little higher than we would like it to be."

"Okay…" I replied. *What is she not saying?*

"When he is better and his virus seems to be gone, we want you to come back in for more blood work so we can check to make sure his white cell count has returned to normal."

"Why?" I asked. "Are you worried that he might have something like…leukemia?" I almost dared not say the word out loud.

"Yes," the doctor replied. "That is what we're worried about. But hopefully, when you come back and have another test, his levels will have returned to normal."

But what if they don't? You can't just call me and tell me my son might have leukemia and then hang up!

As much as I wanted to ask the doctor the three million questions that raced through my mind, I didn't. Instead I kept them to myself, put the phone down and proceeded to do what I did best: worry. For two solid weeks until his follow-up blood test, I was certain that Andy had leukemia.

Fortunately, his white cell count did return to normal after his illness was over. It was just another one of those things that we chalked up to the *mystery* that was Andy. But because of all of his health scares, Bart and I were starting to wonder if maybe two kids were enough for us. After all, we had a girl and a boy. That's what every good American family dreams of having, right? Why press our luck? Andy was worrying me twenty-four hours a day, and I really wasn't ready to add another kid to the mix, so we decided to wait a while before having another child—if we ever would at all.

5

Star Spangled Baby

In October 2004, two months after we moved back to Minnesota, we purchased some land in the country. Bart was going to spend that next summer building us a house. I figured that if I were to have another child, I would at least want to wait another year, so the house would be finished. That way Bart would be available to help me with the older two children while I tended to the baby.

Apparently, no one was paying attention when I announced my plans because by the end of October, we found out that we were expecting our third child. My due date was June 30. At first I was a little disappointed with the timing, since the baby would be born right in the middle of summer when Bart would be busy building the house. But it didn't take long before I was just plain excited about the new addition to our family. Besides, Andy was doing okay—and I was too—after we had survived his cancer scare.

With my due date being June 30, and a history of both going past my due date *and* having my babies on special dates, I knew that our baby was going to be born on the Fourth of July. It was the one day that I did *not* want the baby to be born, but for some reason I felt it had already been decided. I was sad that our child would always be cheated out of his birthday, always having to go to a parade or family picnic on his real birthday and having to have his birthday party on an alternate date. Sure enough, at around 11:00 p.m. on July 3, my contractions started. I knew there was no way I would have the baby within the next 59 minutes, so I resigned myself to the fact that I would have a Fourth of July baby.

At 5:30 the next morning (July Fourth, in case I forgot to mention that little detail), Ethan Robert Johnson was born. He reminded me a lot of Emma, except that he had huge, round eyes. At birth, of course, they were dark bluish-gray, but over time they developed into the most beautiful bright blue. Out of all of our children, Ethan was definitely the most easy-going as a baby. He fit right into our little family, and it didn't take long for me to feel like he had always been there—the same way it had been with the other two kids. It was hard to imagine what life was like before any of them were part of the family.

One night in August 2005, something very strange happened. I almost hesitate to mention it because I don't really understand it, but it is so important to the story that I cannot leave it out. I was sitting in bed, reading a book before I fell asleep, and Bart was looking at house plans. Suddenly, I *heard* in my head these exact words: "By this time next year you will not have all of your children."

I looked around the room. *What? Who said that? Did I just think those words in my mind or did I hear them? Why would I think something like that? Was it God? If it was God, why would he word it like that? Or was it Satan, trying to scare me?*

This was the first time anything like this had ever happened to me. Sure, I had felt the Lord leading me in a certain direction before. I had felt *divine nudgings* a time or two. And there were definitely times that I believed the Holy Spirit was trying to tell me something specific. But this was different. This was verbal—and audible.

I looked over at Bart, and I could tell by the fact that he was still engrossed in his book that he hadn't heard anything. I considered telling him about the words but decided against it, as if speaking them out loud would make them come true. I kept those words to myself until several months later when I finally confided in my pastor's wife, who is also a trusted friend and mentor. She told me that God does not instill in us a spirit of fear, and because I was certainly made fearful by those words, they must not have come from the Lord. I figured then that it must have been Satan.

My pastor's wife went on to say that Satan does not know the future; he only tells lies and tries to intimidate us and render us ineffective for God's kingdom. If he can distract us using something that he knows will scare us, he will. I still wasn't sure. Something inside me felt that it was God. How could Satan speak audibly inside my head? It was actually rather embarrassing to admit that after almost fifteen years of walking with the Lord, I couldn't tell the difference between God's voice, Satan's voice, and my own imagination. Shouldn't it be as easy as telling night from day?

These words haunted me for some time. I had always had a fear of losing the people closest to me. When I was little, my biggest fear was that my mother would die and I would have to live with my grandparents or one of my aunts, since my dad was sick and couldn't take care of me. Somewhere around 1999 my biggest fear became Y2K, but we all know how that turned out. Then I got married, and all of my fears of my mother dying transferred over to Bart. If he was ever late coming home from work or a day of hunting, I would be standing at the window, watching for his car with the phone in my hand, ready to call the sheriff at any moment to report him missing.

But then I had kids. Before that I didn't even know the meaning of the word *worry*. I just knew that I wouldn't want to live if something were to happen to one of my children. So when I heard those words in my head that night, my fears went soaring to new heights. It was all I could think about. I kept wondering what it meant—was one of my children going to die? By the time next August rolled around, would one of them be gone? Which one?

Over that next year, I would find myself staring at my children's pictures, trying to imagine my life without each of them, one at a time. Which one would be the hardest to live without? Obviously, there was no answer to that question; I loved them all and needed them all in my life. Sometimes at night I would rock Ethan to sleep in his room, imagining what it would be like if that were the last time I would ever rock him. What if he died and I had to sit in that same rocking chair with empty arms? The thoughts consumed me and I finally had to tell Bart about the voice I had heard. He also dismissed it as my overactive imagination—which wasn't really that much of a stretch—or my fears getting the best of me. I hoped he was right, but part of me still feared that he wasn't.

My relationship with God was still floundering. After five years of marriage spent wondering how I, as a married woman, fit into God's plan without feeling like I was just my husband's little side-kick, I started to feel more and more distant from God. I felt like my internship was the last time that I had really been used in a ministry role, and that bothered me because I thought I had been called into full-time ministry. I doubted whether or not I even played a part in God's master plan anymore, and I didn't know what to do to feel close to him again.

That September, Andy had tubes put in his ears. Now every time he had an ear infection, which was still just as often, we were able to treat just the ear, using medicated drops, rather than treating his whole body with oral antibiotics. I felt much better about this. I was already concerned with the amount of antibiotics he had consumed in his young life. We also noticed another change occur with the placement of the tubes: Andy's speech began to improve. He had lived most of his little life with fluid constantly surrounding his eardrum, which continually became infected. This fluid made hearing difficult. The doctor compared Andy to someone who was listening to another person talking underwater—all he could make out were muffled sounds. This did not help him at all during the formative years when he was learning to speak. When Andy spoke, he said no beginning or ending consonants, although the middle vowel sounds and intonations were correct. When the tubes were placed in his ears, the fluid was finally allowed to drain out and Andy could hear perfectly—and we could finally understand what he was saying! Things finally seemed to be improving on the health front.

Bart had finished up the house enough for us to finally move in on October 4, 2005. We packed up our belongings and moved ten miles out of town to our new home. The next day, we took off for Ohio to visit my grandfather, who had been diagnosed with stage-four colon cancer and was told he had only a few months to live. Since most of my Ohio relatives had not yet met Ethan, I thought it was important for us to go there so that all of them, especially my grandpa, could see him.

The rest of the winter went along pretty uneventfully, health-wise. Andy and Ethan both had some kind of cold virus around Christmastime. The cough that accompanied this particular virus was the kind that made me want to scrape my fingernails down a chalkboard just so I could hear something more soothing! I brought Ethan with me to the church women's Christmas party one night, and he started coughing. All at once, everyone stopped what they were doing and stared at me, as if to say, "Get that kid to a doctor!"

I just smiled and said, "Oh, Andy had this when he was little. It sounds scary, but it's okay." Ethan was so congested that when he coughed he threw up all of his milk, just as Andy had done when he was four months old. So obviously, it didn't scare me. There was nothing Ethan could throw at me that I hadn't seen before.

In February, Ethan developed RSV, which is a common respiratory virus that can cause breathing complications for young children. We went to the doctor, and she sent us home with a nebulizer and some Albuterol to help Ethan breathe easier. I think we only used the nebulizer twice. Ethan sailed smoothly through RSV with no complications—and I thought RSV was supposed to be life-threatening.

We were now six months into the year after I heard those horrible words in my head, and nothing horrible had happened. Maybe everyone was right; maybe it was just my imagination. Maybe it was just the devil doing what he did best: using my worst fear to get me so sidetracked that I wasn't any good to anybody. Perhaps all three of the kids really were going to be fine and there was never any reason to worry. Now if we could just make it to August again, I could finally exhale and breathe a sigh of relief!

6

You Give and Take Away

On the last Sunday in February 2006, Bart and I had Ethan dedicated to the Lord in the morning church service, just as we had done with Emma and Andy when they were younger. Bart and I, along with our three children, stood in front of the congregation during Ethan's little dedication ceremony. Our pastor held Ethan and asked us to repeat after him as he told the Lord that we wanted Ethan's life to be used for his glory. By dedicating Ethan, we were saying to the Lord that we would not stand in the way of our little baby being used by him for his eternal purposes, no matter how he may choose to do so.

But to me it always seemed like we were rushing things a little. After all, this was only a little baby we were talking about. He was ours for now. What we were saying God could do wouldn't even happen until years in the future. During each of my children's dedications, I remember standing there and thinking the same thing: *For now, our child is only a baby. Let us raise him and take care of him; let him be a kid, and then you can have him, Lord—to do whatever you want with his life…as long as you don't call him to the jungles of Africa. And please don't call him to be a martyr. Oh, and please let him live to be ninety years old.*

Ethan's dedication was no different. As I stood in the front of the church, repeating after the pastor, I was thinking, *Okay God, you can have Ethan, and you can do whatever you want with his life—as long as you check with me first and I say it's okay.* Believe me; I definitely would not have okayed what God was planning for Ethan if I had been given the opportunity. Unfortunately for me, God doesn't have to check with me before doing anything with his children, because that is exactly what they are: his children—not mine. That can be one hard lesson for any parent to learn.

During the weeks following Ethan's dedication, the words that I had heard that past summer were playing over and over in the background of my mind. Something about that dedication ceremony triggered the words that I had almost forgotten about after several months of nothing earth-shattering happening to my family.

Bart had spent most of the previous fall and winter finishing up the house in his spare time. He hung the siding on the outside of the house in November. In February, he nailed up the trim around the doors and windows. Our stairs were going to be solid oak, but for now they were made of scrap two-by-fours that Bart painted with some mis-tinted, purplish-brown paint that he got at the hardware store on clearance. This way the *real* stairs wouldn't get ruined by drywall mud and work boots going up and down them constantly. The fireplace wasn't in yet, so there was a huge cement slab in the living room with a black fireplace insert sitting on top, covered in clear plastic sheeting and drywall dust. The house was *mostly* done. Our building loan allowed one year from the start of our building project to its completion. That one-year period was up in the end of March, and we had a meeting with the building inspector scheduled for March 30, 2006.

But March ended up being a very *interesting* month to say the least. Somewhere around the middle of March, Ethan got yet another virus, followed by an ear infection, and I took him to see the doctor. Actually, this time I didn't take him to see his regular doctor; I went to someone else. I was trying to see different doctors every time Ethan was sick so that our regular pediatrician didn't think I was a paranoid, hypochondriac mother. The doctor we saw this particular time, who was actually a friend from church, said that he had been seeing a lot of kids with high fevers that week, and it was probably a virus that would just have to run its course. But for the ear infection he prescribed antibiotics.

After two days on antibiotics, Ethan still had a fever—only now it had reached 105°. Andy had already had several 105-degree fevers before, so again, I wasn't *too* worried. However, I was also used to antibiotics magically working within the first twelve hours or so. These weren't helping at all, so I took Ethan back to the doctor. This time I had to go to the emergency room because it was Sunday, and the clinic was closed. The doctor in the ER switched Ethan to a different antibiotic hoping that it would help.

On Monday, I called the ENT (ear, nose and throat) specialist that had put Andy's tubes in and told him that Ethan was now having his fifth ear infection in almost nine months. The doctor agreed that because of his many infections, Ethan would be a candidate for tubes as well. I scheduled an appointment for a consultation with the ENT specialist on May 2. Finally I felt some relief. At least *something* would change for the better, and we wouldn't have to play "antibiotic roulette" every time Ethan got an ear infection.

That night, March 20, was our church talent show. Emma and I performed a duet. We sang "I've got the Joy," plus another song. I remember that night vividly (except for the name of the second song). Ethan was very lethargic and continued to run a high fever despite the Tylenol and Motrin I had been giving him. He just wanted to lie around and had no sparkle in his eyes. There was not even the smallest hint of the jovial little personality I was used to seeing. He didn't smile; he didn't laugh. I knew all along that he was sick, but now I was starting to get really worried.

That night I was up constantly with Ethan. He wouldn't let me put him down. When I held him he was okay, but as soon as I laid him in his crib he would cry. So, I *slept* (and I use that term loosely) with him in my bed all night. By morning his condition had not improved, and he seemed to have developed several tiny purple spots on his earlobes that weren't there before. His fever was still 105°, and he was extremely fussy. The new antibiotics didn't seem to be working, either. I also noticed that his hands, feet, and lips looked a little blue, so I decided to bring him back to the clinic. It was a Tuesday and the clinic was open, but I didn't have time to wait for an appointment; I went straight to the emergency room. This time I was going to ask if the doctor would give Ethan an antibiotic shot that would work instantly and give him some relief from this terrible infection.

I called my mother-in-law, who lived five miles away, to come and stay at my house with Emma and Andy. When she arrived I took off for the hospital with Ethan.

When I got to the ER and got Ethan registered, a nurse came into our room and took some vitals. The ER doctor came in to see Ethan, and I told her that I wanted an antibiotic shot to make the ear infection go away faster. She looked in his ears and said the ear infection was already gone.

"Then why is his fever still so high?" I asked.

The doctor shook her head. "Could still be the virus," she replied. "Have you been giving him Tylenol for his fever?"

"Yes," I answered.

"Well, sometimes Tylenol can build up in a person's system and cause symptoms like this," she said. She also gave me several other theories.

Great. Had I done this to Ethan by trying to lower his fever? I thought I only gave him the recommended dose of Tylenol and no more. I felt sick to my stomach. The doctor ordered blood work to check Ethan's liver functions, white cell count, and a few other things. We were sent to a different room, and I sat on the bed with Ethan and waited for the results of the blood test to come back. About fifteen minutes later, the ER doctor returned to the room, followed by our regular pediatrician. I was surprised to see her since she wasn't normally in the ER. I looked straight into our doctor's eyes and asked, "Is it bad?"

She shook her head. "Yes. He's septic."

I didn't know what that meant. "Was it the Tylenol?"

"No." Our doctor explained that the viral infection had gone into Ethan's blood stream and was spreading throughout his body. It was more than the doctors in our local hospital were comfortable dealing with, so they planned to send us to St. Mary's Hospital in Duluth by ambulance.

Duluth? I hadn't brought anything with me for an overnight stay. I had only the clothes on my back and maybe one extra diaper for Ethan. What about my mother-in-law at my house with Emma and Andy? Could she stay there with them for a long time? I didn't know what her schedule was like.

At this time I still didn't fully grasp how serious our situation was. Otherwise, I would not have been fretting over the little details. I called my mother-in-law to tell her the situation. I also called Bart at work and told him we were going to Duluth, and I must have called church to have Ethan put on the prayer chain.

Soon the paramedics arrived, ready to prep Ethan for his ambulance trip to Duluth. They tried to get an IV started, but they were having trouble finding a vein that they could access because Ethan was starting to get dehydrated. I sat right next to him, holding his hand as they inserted a catheter into his bladder and decided to run the IV line through his jugular vein as a last resort. While the paramedics were working on Ethan, my pastor showed up in the doorway (which is why I think I must have called the church). He stood there and watched quietly while Ethan was being loaded onto a gurney to be taken into the ambulance. I walked outside with my pastor and we talked for a minute.

"Did your wife tell you about the voice I heard last summer?" I asked.

"Yes, she did."

"I think it's happening—I think this is it," I said.

My pastor went on to tell me that he didn't think that the words meant what I thought they meant. Since Bart and I had recently dedicated Ethan to the Lord, my pastor suggested that maybe the words meant something about Ethan dying to the world, or dying to sin; or maybe that *we,* meaning Bart and I, didn't *have* him anymore because he now belonged to the Lord. Nobody wanted to admit that maybe the words meant what they sounded like—maybe one of our kids was actually going to die, and maybe it was going to be our baby.

7

"Not Much Worries Me..."

I rode along in the ambulance with Ethan. I sat on the gurney holding him in my lap while the paramedics pumped fluids and antibiotics through his IV and put an oxygen mask over his face. It was my first time in an ambulance, but for some reason, the novelty wore off rather quickly. We even drove right past our driveway en route to Duluth, which probably would have been fun under different circumstances.

I glanced behind me at the paramedic who was driving, then down at the speedometer, and noted that we were traveling at ninety miles an hour. I hoped the paramedic was a good driver.

Please, Lord, don't let us get into an accident. That's the last thing we need right now.

When we arrived at St. Mary's Hospital in Duluth (in record time, I might add), Ethan was taken for more tests, and I was sent to a room to wait for a doctor. As I looked out the door of our room and into the bigger, more open area where the nurse's station was located, I saw the bed that Andy had been in when he was in this same hospital for his MRI. I remembered the feeling that I had gotten that I would be here again—and here I was—only I wasn't with Andy, as I had once thought I would be; I was with Ethan.

When Ethan was done with his tests, the nurse brought him back to the room and gave him to me to hold on the hospital bed. Not long after that, Bart showed up.

"How did you get here so fast?" I asked him.

"I was at home getting ready to leave when I heard the ambulance go by. I figured it was you. I wasn't far behind." Bart waited with me until the doctor came in to talk to us.

When the doctor finally came into the room, he explained that he had looked over the paperwork and lab results and had examined Ethan himself. I will never forget what he said next: "I have been a doctor for many years and I have seen a lot of things, and not much worries me. But I am *very* worried about Ethan."

That is not the kind of thing any parent wants to hear. Something like: "He'll be fine; don't worry," would have been better. The doctor told us that it looked to him as though Ethan's liver was failing. He said he didn't know exactly what was going on inside Ethan's body, and he would feel more comfortable sending him somewhere where there was a liver specialist. He ordered Ethan to be air-lifted to the University of Minnesota Medical Center in Minneapolis. I asked if I could go in the helicopter with Ethan, but I was told that Bart and I would have to drive down by ourselves. Because the pilot and several nurses would be traveling with Ethan in the helicopter, there wouldn't be any room for us. This was definitely much more than I had expected when I left the house that morning.

I quickly got on a computer in the waiting room and sent out an urgent e-mail to everyone on my contact list and a few other people whom Bart knew. It said something like this:

Tuesday, March 21, 2006
Please pray for Ethan. We are in the hospital in Duluth, and the doctor said he is very worried about him. I don't know what is wrong with him. We are on our way to the U of M, and I'm not sure if Ethan will survive until we get there. Please pray. Jessica

Bart and I waited until Ethan was loaded onto the helicopter before heading to the parking deck to get our car. I knew we could not drive as fast as a helicopter could fly, and I was scared to death that Ethan would be gone before we could get to Minneapolis. As we drove, we could see the helicopter in the sky; but eventually, it went out of sight. That was the scariest moment of my life up to that point. I had never felt so out of control. I had always done everything I could to protect my children, and now I could do nothing. Bart and I prayed, but the drive to Minneapolis would take more than two hours. I don't even remember how we made it through that trip.

When we arrived at the University of Minnesota Medical Center, we found out where Ethan was and headed up the elevator to unit 5B: pediatric intensive care. There we were met by the liver specialist. He told us that after examining Ethan, he was pretty sure that Ethan's liver was not going to fail. He explained to us that livers are very resilient, and even if part of Ethan's liver was damaged and had to be removed, he could live with what was left. The liver doctor figured something else was going on that needed to be dealt with, so he passed us on to the pediatric hematology/oncology specialists.

Later, after more tests had been done, the pediatric hematologist, Dr. Kumar, and one of his fellows came to talk with us. They sat us down and explained that they still weren't exactly sure what was going on with Ethan, but from the looks of his lab results, it was most likely one of three things: a bad virus, leukemia, or something called HLH. The bad virus scared me because I knew that anti-viral drugs did not work the same as antibiotics, and growing a culture to determine just which virus was infecting Ethan could take some time. I didn't know how much time Ethan had. The leukemia was also scary, but I had almost expected one of my kids to have leukemia after Andy's little scare. Also, I knew that not everyone with leukemia died. The HLH was a little more serious.

Dr. Kumar explained that HLH (Hemophagocytic lymphohistiocytosis) was a rare disease in which the immune system reacts to a foreign invader, such as a virus, by sending out a type of white blood cell called a histiocyte to fight it. When the virus is gone, there is a malfunction in the body's ability to *turn off* the histiocytes. Instead, the body sends out more and more histiocytes, which then go on to destroy bodily tissues and organs, such as the liver and spleen. Doctor Kumar explained that there are two forms of HLH: the genetic form and the secondary form. The genetic form (Familial HLH) usually presents itself during infancy, when a child is fighting one of his or her first illnesses. The secondary form is not caused by a genetic defect; it is instead triggered by some other underlying disorder.

If Ethan had the genetic form of HLH, the only cure was chemotherapy, followed by a bone marrow transplant. If a bone marrow transplant was not done, then HLH would likely return with the next viral infection, and the whole process would begin all over again. The one thing that puzzled the doctors was how Ethan had lived nine months without developing HLH sooner, especially since he had been sick many times before.

After hearing the doctor's description of HLH, and adding that to my fears of an unstoppable killer virus, I casually said to someone that maybe the best of the three diagnoses was leukemia (as if any of the three could be called "the best"). Somehow my comment got onto an e-mail, and then people were forwarding e-mails to their friends saying, "Please pray that it's leukemia."

I wanted to scream, "Don't do that!" This is when we were introduced to the CaringBridge website. Thank goodness. It was getting difficult to respond to all of the different e-mails and get the word out to everyone without the story getting screwed up so badly. We were relieved to be able to have one source of information to keep everyone updated on Ethan's condition. There were several computers right outside of Ethan's room in the hallway of the PICU, so whenever we received any new information, we went straight to CaringBridge and updated our journal.

That night Bart and I tried to sleep in Ethan's room, but there was only one chair. In the pediatric intensive care unit, there is a nurse in the room twenty-four hours a day, so we felt comfortable enough to leave Ethan for the night and go to the family lounge and try to sleep there on a couch. We got to the family lounge at about ten o'clock at night, and it was packed. Every couch was taken, and I ended up in a recliner. I don't even remember where Bart slept. Some woman was watching television until one o'clock in the morning. How were we supposed to get any sleep? I felt like yelling, "My son is lying in a hospital bed fighting for his life, and you're watching the History Channel? Come on!" But there was no use getting upset. Still, something would have to change or we would become walking zombies due to lack of sleep.

We had put our names on the waiting list for a room at the Ronald McDonald House, but I wasn't sure if I wanted to stay there since it was several blocks away from the hospital. I didn't think I could be that far away from Ethan. But after a few nights in the family lounge, I quickly changed my mind. When we were told that a room with a set of bunk beds, a queen bed, and a fold-out couch would soon be available for us at the Ronald McDonald House, we snatched it up without hesitation.

The next day, March 23, the doctors had enough results from the blood tests to determine that Ethan did indeed have HLH. Whether it was the primary (genetic) form or the secondary form, which was triggered by some other underlying condition, was yet to be determined. DNA samples had been sent off to a lab in Cincinnati that specialized in HLH, to see if Ethan had one of the four known genetic defects for the disease, but the results would take several weeks. Doctor Kumar also explained that Ethan could have a brand new genetic defect for HLH, although that was less likely. For now, the plan was to start chemotherapy, which was necessary to kill the histiocytes and stop the HLH from further damaging Ethan's organs no matter which form of the disease he had.

That morning Ethan had a lumbar puncture, a bone marrow biopsy, a chest CT scan—which showed that he also had a slight pneumonia—and he had a Hickman catheter (double-lumen line) inserted into a vein in his chest that went directly into his heart. With this the doctors could pump more than one medication or fluid into Ethan's body at a time, and the lab technicians wouldn't have to constantly poke his veins for blood tests. Because of the damage to his liver, Ethan's platelet count was low and his blood was not clotting as quickly as it should. This explained the tiny purple spots that I had seen on Ethan's earlobes, which now covered his entire body. They were called *petechiae*, and they were actually small dots of blood in his skin, which were caused by capillaries that had hemorrhaged due to the low platelet count. Ethan's blood-clotting impairment also caused him to bleed at the site of his Hickman catheter for eighteen hours. This became a concern.

On Friday, March 24, we were able to move into our room at the Ronald McDonald House. This was a huge blessing. Even if I wasn't able to be away from Ethan for long, it was a place where we could stash our things, take a shower, and eat. There were three meals provided each day, and we were only asked to pay a small daily fee. It was well worth it. Bart's parents and sister came to the hospital with Emma and Andy, and we all stayed at the Ronald McDonald House that night. I hadn't seen Emma and Andy since I left them with Bart's mom and took Ethan to the ER back home. It felt good to have everyone together again. We spent the evening touring the expansive Ronald McDonald House. Emma and Andy really enjoyed playing in the game room and running around in the outdoor playground. They referred to the Ronald McDonald House as the "hotel." If only we were actually there on vacation!

On March 25, Ethan started his chemo treatments, which seemed to be going well, and he had no side effects that we noticed. That morning his eyes were open for the first time since we were in Duluth. He seemed very alert, even if it was only for a few minutes. To me it seemed like a noticeable improvement. Unfortunately, the bleeding had continued from his Hickman site. It had been bleeding for forty-eight hours straight and it seemed to be getting worse. Bart and I had to take turns standing next to Ethan's crib, pressing two fingers to his chest—one on each side of the tube—trying to put pressure on it to stop the bleeding. Meanwhile, he was receiving clotting factors from plasma through his IV. If the bleeding did not stop, the doctors would have to take the catheter out and place a new one in a different site, which would be another surgery. They explained to us that it wouldn't exactly be ideal to perform any kind of surgery on Ethan when his clotting time was slow. Bart and I took turns pressing on the tube in Ethan's chest for a total of four hours, hoping that the bleeding would eventually stop on its own.

By that evening, Ethan's liver started to show signs of improvement. It seemed to be producing its own clotting factors, and his bleeding also seemed to be slowing down. By 5:30 the next morning, the bleeding had completely stopped. We were thankful beyond words. Because the bleeding complication was out of the way, the doctors said that Ethan would possibly be able to move out of the PICU the next day and into a regular room. This was indeed a good sign.

8

Andy's Cough

On Sunday, March 26, Emma, Andy, Bart's parents and his sister were getting ready to head back up north. We ate lunch together at the Ronald McDonald House before they left. Many of the families at the Ronald McDonald House were there because their children were fighting cancer or undergoing a bone marrow transplant for a rare genetic disease. It was simply understood that if you were sick, you were to wear a mask to cover your nose and mouth to protect those around you whose immune systems may be compromised. There was also a hand sanitizer pump located on just about every wall. We had quickly gotten into the habit of constantly sanitizing our hands since Ethan had started chemotherapy. Even though the doctors had not received his genetic test results, they were proceeding as if he did have the genetic form of HLH and needed a bone marrow transplant. Because of this, and because it was the only way to stop the histiocytes from multiplying, one of the medicines in Ethan's "chemo cocktail" was an immune-suppressant, and it made him very vulnerable to infection.

While we were eating in the dining room of the Ronald McDonald House, Andy started coughing. I did notice that his cough sounded a little worse than just an average, everyday cough, but I didn't even have a chance to give it a second thought because a woman came out of nowhere from another table and handed me a child-sized face mask with Mickey Mouse on it.

"He needs to wear one of these," she said. "There are a lot of kids in this house who can't afford to be around someone who is sick. If he's going to be here, he needs a mask. I'm just telling you what anyone else would tell you."

It was as if she were saying, "Hey, I know you're new around here, so I'll let you off easy this time. Next time you won't be so lucky."

I thanked her for the mask and put it on Andy's face, not quite sure how he was going to finish his lunch with it on.

As nice as it was to see Emma and Andy, it was actually a relief when they headed back home with Bart's parents. I felt like I could only handle so much time away from Ethan, and the kids couldn't really be around him—especially Andy, who seemed to have some kind of virus, as usual. I tried my best to balance my time between having "fun" at the Ronald McDonald House with my two older kids, and sitting in Ethan's hospital room wondering whether or not he was going to get better. Once Emma and Andy were on their way back home, I devoted all of my energy to worrying about Ethan.

Later that day, Ethan was moved from the PICU to the pediatric hematology/oncology ward which was located one floor up. This move was tougher for me than I had expected. Initially, I thought it was a good thing because it meant that Ethan was improving. But the lack of a nurse in the room with Ethan twenty-four hours a day really caused me great concern. I felt like anything could happen while the nurses were out of the room—which they seemed to be often—so I stayed in the room at all times and refused to leave, not even for meals.

That night my parents arrived from Ohio. They hadn't seen Ethan since he was admitted to the hospital, and they were planning on spending some time with him and then heading north to spend a few days visiting Emma and Andy at Bart's parents' house.

Ethan's blood oxygen levels started to drop slightly, so he was put on oxygen. Bart slept in Ethan's hospital room so I could try to get some sleep at the Ronald McDonald House.

In the morning, after sleeping in a chair all night, Bart made an entry in our CaringBridge journal about watching the sunrise with Ethan. It would be the first of several entries about how thankful Bart was to get one more day with Ethan—one more sunrise. Bart was still able to find things to be thankful for in the midst of our circumstances. He was still holding on to some hope that Ethan would get better and eventually be able to come home. I, on the other hand, was finding it increasingly difficult to remain positive. I began doubting whether or not Ethan would ever get better.

By Wednesday, March 29, Ethan was starting to become more alert. He was even starting to get up and crawl in his crib. Bart called it "doing push-ups." I was starting to worry that he would fall right out of his crib if his energy levels kept improving as they had been.

Bart was planning on heading back home the next day to spend some *normal* time at our house with the kids. Emma and Andy had been staying with their grandparents for a week now, and Bart figured they'd like to be at home for a while.

Although Ethan was starting to become more active and seemed to be improving, he had developed a slight fever of 101.5° that wasn't responding to Tylenol. The doctors weren't sure if the fever was from some kind of infection, or if Ethan's body was simply reacting to the low white cell count caused by the chemotherapy. Regardless of the cause of the fever, Ethan's doctors decided to switch his antibiotics to something stronger.

Bart never made it back home to visit the kids because sometime later that day, we got some interesting news from Bart's mom: she had taken Andy to see our regular pediatrician because he was getting sicker. His cough was getting worse, he had a high fever, and he just wasn't himself. The doctor did an X-ray and found that Andy had developed pneumonia. She wanted to admit Andy into the hospital, but with Bart and me in Minneapolis, she didn't think it would be ideal to have Andy alone in a hospital three hours away from his parents. So our doctor called the U of M to see if they would admit Andy and we could all be together.

I still remember one of the nurses on the hematology/oncology floor rolling her eyes. "That's just what we need," she said. "All of our beds are full. We don't have room for another kid, especially one who only has pneumonia. They're just overreacting." That nurse had been one of my favorite nurses, until then.

When Bart's mom and my parents (who had been at the Johnsons', visiting the kids) arrived late that night with Andy, he was admitted into the hospital, and his room was three doors down from Ethan's. His labs showed that his liver functions were also elevated, but that could have been because he was fighting an infection. In the CaringBridge journal, Bart wrote:

> *Although the doctors are being extremely cautious by sending Andy down here, I assume he will be released tomorrow.*

I think we were all feeling a little embarrassed by our doctor's insistence upon Andy being in Minneapolis with us and by what seemed to be extremely overcautious handling of his health care. Nevertheless, I was glad that he was close by. I don't know what I would have done if Andy was in a hospital over three hours away from us.

By Thursday morning, it was looking as if maybe our doctor back home wasn't overreacting after all. The doctors at the university decided that Andy should undergo all of the same tests that Ethan had for HLH. Bart took Andy down to the surgery ward to have a bone marrow biopsy, but the doctors there postponed it until later because his pneumonia was pretty severe, and he wouldn't have been a good candidate for anesthesia.

At this time I started to feel like my life was unraveling at both ends. I had gotten used to the fact that Ethan was sick. Things were going along at a steady pace, and he seemed to be recovering slowly. I had gotten a pretty good grasp of the disease that he had and what it would take for him to recover. But when Andy showed up at the hospital with similar symptoms only a week later, I almost lost it. What in the world was going on? Were we under some kind of spiritual attack?

It wasn't just Bart and I who were thrown off course by Andy's sudden illness; Andy's doctors were thrown for a loop as well. If Andy and Ethan both had HLH, then they must have the genetic form. It would be too unlikely that they would both develop the secondary form at the same time. But why wouldn't Andy have developed HLH sooner in his little life? It usually showed up with one of the first illnesses or serious infections in a child's life, and Andy had already had two and a half years of constant serious infections. The doctors had never heard of anything like this happening before. But if it were actually the secondary form of HLH, what was the trigger? Secondary HLH rarely showed up in brothers at the same time. It was a mystery.

To make matters worse, even though Andy was now in the same hospital as Ethan, I still couldn't go to his room to see him. Because Ethan was undergoing chemotherapy and his immune system was severely compromised, he could not come in contact with Andy's germs. Andy was obviously sick with some kind of virus, and I was not allowed to go from one boy's room to the other's. I had to choose one child to stay with and not see the other. How could I pick which child to stay with? I wanted to be with both, and Andy was asking for me, too. It about tore my heart in two not to be able to be with him when he was so sick, especially since I knew he needed me.

I decided to stay with Ethan because in my mind he was still more seriously ill, and I didn't know how much time we would have with him. Bart's mom, who had been taking care of Andy at her home when he developed the pneumonia, stayed with him. Bart floated back and forth, only standing just inside the boys' rooms, making sure he didn't come too close to either of them. He didn't want to pass any viruses to Ethan from Andy. All of us had to wear hospital gowns and masks whenever we were around either of the boys, and we had to change into new gowns if we entered the other boy's room.

The infectious disease doctors visited Andy's room and explained to Bart that there were four different viruses that could cause pneumonia and also affect the liver and produce test results similar to those from HLH. I don't remember which viruses those were, but the hope was that maybe Andy just had a virus that produced HLH-like blood test results, and it was just a coincidence that he had gotten that virus at the same time that his brother had developed HLH.

No such luck. On Friday afternoon, March 31, Andy was ready for his spinal tap and bone marrow biopsy. He also had to have a central line put in, just as Ethan had. After he came out of surgery, Andy was placed in the pediatric intensive care unit. The pneumonia had begun to get much worse, and he was placed on a ventilator with a breathing tube inserted into his lungs. Every once in a while, the nurses would come in and suction fluid out of Andy's lungs. It was so hard to see my little boy, who only a few days ago had come to the hospital to visit his brother, now lying in a hospital bed of his own with a blue breathing tube taped to his mouth, completely unconscious. I had reached my breaking point long before this, and it was only by the grace of God that I was still functioning at all.

The doctors took cultures of the fluid from Andy's lungs and had it sent down to the lab. At this time his blood tests were showing that he did, in fact, have the initial stages of HLH. Some of the cultures that had been taken from Ethan when he first arrived had grown enough to determine that the virus he had which may have started all of this was called *Adenovirus*. The doctors were going to proceed to treat Andy as if he also had Adenovirus. In a way, it was helpful to Andy that Ethan had gotten sick a week earlier. Otherwise, Andy may not have survived long enough for his own virus cultures to grow and for the virus to be properly identified.

We were told that Adenovirus was a common virus that would usually cause a person to develop pinkeye, and sometimes even pneumonia. Occasionally, it could make a person very sick, but had it ever been known to trigger secondary HLH? There were still some pieces missing to this puzzle, and we were quickly running out of time to find the answers.

9

The "Aha" Moment

By Saturday, April 1, we had the missing piece to the puzzle—and a diagnosis. Several of Andy's test results had come back and revealed that Andy, and most likely Ethan also, had a genetic immune deficiency disease called X-Linked Agammaglobulinemia (XLA). The main defect in XLA is the inability of pre-B-lymphocytes to mature into B-lymphocytes, or B-cells. Without B-cells, XLA patients cannot produce antibodies, which are the body's first line of defense against certain microorganisms such as bacteria, viruses, and fungi.[2] This explained so much, like why Andy had gotten sick so often, even though he and Emma were always exposed to the same germs, and Emma almost never got sick. Andy never had any of his own antibodies, other than the ones he got from me during pregnancy and breastfeeding. Once those began to disappear, he simply got sick all the time.

The doctors were pretty sure that Ethan also had XLA, although it never showed up on his test results because the HLH was so advanced that all of his white cell counts were low. An absence of B-cells wouldn't have set off any alarms or red flags.

It made sense that Ethan would also have XLA because he seemed to be beginning the cycle of having one infection after another, just like Andy. Now that Ethan was almost nine months old, the antibodies he received from me were starting to disappear. The diagnosis of XLA meant that Ethan did not have genetic HLH, but rather, secondary HLH. Because of the lack of antibodies in his system, the Adenovirus was allowed to spread and take over very quickly, making him very sick. While Adenovirus alone may not have triggered HLH, Adenovirus combined with XLA could.

This was good news for Ethan, who was being prepared for a bone marrow transplant. He would continue with the chemotherapy to kill the rest of the histiocytes and stop the HLH, but after the treatments were finished, he would not need the bone marrow transplant. Instead, we were told that he and Andy would receive monthly intravenous infusions of immunoglobulins (IgG) to replace the antibodies that their bodies lacked.

At first, I was overjoyed. *Yea! No bone marrow transplant! My sons will live!* But Bart was more realistic. He previously had the notion that when and if the boys left the hospital, it would be because they were cured—done. Now when they left, they would have a life-long struggle to overcome infections, even with the help of the infusions. There would always be that increased risk of complications; they would never be completely healthy.

Although this diagnosis caused a slight setback in our positive outlook for the future, we eventually came to terms with the new reality we were faced with, and then proceeded to focus on the boys getting better. They both still had a long way to go. Ethan had started to grow increasingly fussy during the previous twenty-four hours and would be having an MRI to make sure that his fussiness was just a reaction to the aches and pains caused by the chemotherapy and nothing more. Meanwhile, Andy was still on a breathing tube. His pneumonia was still so bad that the doctors weren't sure if he would be able to breathe on his own.

By Sunday, April 2, we had a little bit of good news about Andy: his pneumonia appeared to be slightly improving, and we were hopeful that his breathing tube would come out the next day. He never officially developed full-blown HLH and would not need to start chemotherapy. He and Ethan were receiving high doses of immunoglobulins and an anti-viral drug called Cidofovir to fight the virus.

Ethan, on the other hand, was not improving. His fussiness continued, and he now seemed to be retaining fluid. The anti-viral drug he was getting through his IV was known to be hard on the kidneys, so it was taken with a liter of fluid to protect the kidneys. Ethan's body was not able to shed this extra fluid. He had retained the full liter, and most of it was collecting in his abdomen.

I had gone to the Ronald McDonald House for a while because I thought I could finally get some rest. Both of the boys seemed to be holding their own, so I headed down the street to tidy up, maybe do some laundry and take a short nap. But at 2:30 in the afternoon, just as I had lain down to rest, I got a phone call from Bart. He began by telling me not to panic, which was my first clue that something was wrong. He went on to explain that Ethan had been having some trouble breathing because of all the extra fluid in his abdomen. Eventually the nursing staff had to issue a code-blue and place him on a ventilator, just like Andy. Then he was transferred back to pediatric intensive care.

Bart suggested that I just stay at the Ronald McDonald House and get some rest because the doctors were sending Ethan down to radiology to do a chest CT scan to see why he was retaining so much fluid. There was no way I would be able to sleep after what he had just told me, so I bolted out the door, not bothering to wait for a shuttle, and ran through the pouring rain all the way to the hospital. When I got to the fifth floor, dripping wet and out of breath, Ethan was already down in radiology. The only people in the room now were Bart, the nurse, and Andy—sleeping very peacefully—with only the sound of the ventilator in the background.

And that's when the reality of the situation hit me: the boys were now in a double room in the intensive care unit. Andy and Ethan were sharing a room. It was something I had always planned for them, since they were only two years apart in age. While Bart was building our house, I dreamed about filling the bedrooms with children. There were four bedrooms on the second floor; two were larger, and two were smaller. I was pregnant with Ethan, although at the time I didn't know if he would be a boy or a girl. His gender would determine what color I would paint the "big bedroom," and which kids would live in it. It would either be Emma and her little sister or Andy and his little brother. The other big bedroom would be mine and Bart's.

When Ethan was born, the big bedroom got a fresh coat of bright blue paint. My plan was to move Ethan out of the nursery and into the big blue bedroom with Andy when he was around two years old. Then the two of them would grow up to be best buds—sharing a bedroom, having sword fights, and staying up too late at night giggling under their covers. But as I stared at Andy and the empty bed beside him, I realized that this may be the only room they would ever share.

10

Saying Goodbye

Eventually Ethan returned from his CT scan and was placed back in the bed next to Andy's. Even if only for a few hours, they shared a room. If only I would have taken a picture of them together. Unfortunately during this time, things were happening so fast I just wasn't looking farther ahead than the next second, let alone years in the future when I would look back and think, *Now that would have been a good idea.*

At 6:10 p.m. on April 2, Bart sent out this cry for help on CaringBridge:

> *Your prayers for Ethan are urgently requested. He has taken a very serious turn for the worse. His blood clotting factors and liver function are deteriorating rapidly and his kidneys have all but failed. They are going to try and perform dialysis, but his situation is not very good. His blood pressure is also very low. At this time we don't know if Ethan will make it, but we leave it in God's hands to take care of him.*

A team of dialysis technicians had come into the room with a huge dialysis machine and were attempting to take some of the fluid out of Ethan's body, but they couldn't perform dialysis unless his blood pressure was high enough, and it just wasn't. The dialysis doctor and her team just stood there, watching him, checking his blood pressure and shaking their heads. There wasn't much they could do.

In the background, a group of nurses was talking about what they were going to do for dinner that night after they got off work. I wanted to scream at them and tell them to get out of the room if they were going to act like nothing was going on in here. My son was dying. Didn't they have the decency to make their plans somewhere else? Maybe they saw this sort of thing all the time and had grown numb to it; maybe it was just "business as usual" for those who spent every day in the pediatric intensive care unit, but not for me. I was so mad, but was unable to speak up. I just stood there by the head of Ethan's bed and whispered into his ear how much I loved him and how proud I was of him. I told him everything was okay and that he was a good little boy.

I remember earlier in the day I had asked the doctor who was in charge of the intensive care unit to tell me when they had reached the point where there was nothing more they could do. Up until then, the doctors still had a few more tricks up their sleeves. Every time Ethan sent a challenge their way, they had something in their back pockets they could try. But now, the doctor came up to Bart and me and said, "Remember what you asked me to tell you earlier?"

"Yes," we replied.

"Well, it's that time." She meant that there was nothing more they could do, and we needed to call Bart's parents and siblings so they could make it down to the hospital in time to say goodbye. My mother was already there because she had stayed at the Ronald McDonald House to watch Emma.

Meanwhile, the dialysis team was still giving it their best shot. They would need to do dialysis for two to four hours for it to be effective, and they couldn't even get it started. After a while, I looked over at the dialysis doctor and she shrugged her shoulders. She and her team packed up and left the room; they could not perform dialysis.

The doctor from intensive care and our hematologist said they could try something called plasma transfer to try to get Ethan's clotting factors to improve. I'm not sure what good that would have done; the doctors were convinced that even if it worked, it wouldn't save Ethan's life. It would maybe buy him a few hours, but since his body wasn't releasing any fluid, adding plasma products would have made him even more bloated, and his already over-stressed heart could have given out. Bart and I didn't want to put his little body through any more torture. His blood pressure was extremely low, and his heart rate was soaring at 200 beats per minute. We didn't know how much longer his body would hold out, and we certainly didn't want to add any more stress for him to handle.

Bart called his parents and told them to come down so they could say goodbye to Ethan. He explained that they needed to leave as soon as possible since they had a three-hour drive.

I wanted to run and scream; I wanted to cry out to God for mercy, but there were doctors and nurses everywhere. There was nowhere I could go to be alone. I remembered that there was a little conference room down the hall, so I went there hoping that I could get on my face and beg God for Ethan's life. But when I got there, there was a very old woman in the room—at least I think it was a woman. She was very short, with a darker complexion and was quite wrinkled. She did not speak English. I tried explaining to her that my son was dying and that I wanted to be alone and pray, but she just smiled and shook her head and said something in a language I did not understand.

Never in my life had I been more frustrated. I knew Ethan was running out of time. There was absolutely nothing I could do—except pray—yet when I tried, there was nowhere I could go. I felt like Ethan's very survival depended on whether or not I could find somewhere that I could be alone with God and cry out to him, begging him to spare Ethan; yet everywhere I turned I kept running into a brick wall. After a few minutes of unsuccessfully trying to convince the person in the conference room that I needed to be alone, I just gave up and returned to Ethan and Andy's room.

Now that I look back, I wonder why it mattered so much whether or not I was alone. Why didn't I just get on my face in the middle of Ethan's room—or in the middle of the hallway for that matter? What would it have mattered what anyone thought? I'm sure given the circumstances they would have understood. Why didn't I just try harder? Bart's parents and siblings arrived at around 10:30 that night, and we all gathered in the waiting room for one huge group hug and crying session. None of us could really believe what was happening; it was still so unbelievable. Just a few days earlier it seemed like Ethan was improving. The chemotherapy seemed to be helping, and he was more alert than he had been in days. What had gone wrong? After we had all hugged each other, Bart told each of us to write a little message to Ethan in the CaringBridge journal.

After that, it was just a waiting game. Everyone had gotten the chance to go into Ethan's room and say goodbye to him. Emma was getting really tired so she went to sleep in the conference room with some of her aunts. Bart and I were just sitting in the room staring at the monitors, watching for any change. I suddenly felt the urge to contact our on-line prayer warriors who were staying up with us to the very end and ask them to join with me as I begged God for a miracle. It was 1:34 a.m. I remember running to the computer and typing out yet another desperate journal entry:

> I just wanted to say that Ethan is still hanging in there...I am not giving up yet. There is still room for a miracle, until God decides to bring Ethan home. He is still here now, so I will keep praying for him and I hope you all do too.

By 3:59 a.m. on April 3, it was obvious that God wasn't going to grant us that miracle. Ethan was hooked up only to his ventilator. Bart and I were taking turns holding him in a rocking chair. He was very heavy from all of the fluid he had retained. I remember that he weighed around eighteen pounds when we first brought him in, but now he weighed thirty-six. His heart was still beating on its own, although with every beat it was getting slower and slower. I couldn't seem to keep my eyes off the heart monitor and the digital numbers that flashed his heart rate in red before my eyes. As long as there was a number there, he was still alive. The numbers kept creeping closer and closer to zero, and when they finally did reach zero I knew he would be gone. It was torture.

Sometimes it didn't even seem like it was Ethan that I was holding. He looked so different; his skin was yellowish and he was puffy. It seemed like the *real* Ethan wasn't even there anymore. I felt that his soul had left the room long before, and only his body was with us. The only thing that told us he was still alive was the machine that said his heart was still beating. I had a feeling my little boy was already in the presence of the Lord.

Bart took his turn holding Ethan while I made another entry on the website:

> Right now Bart and I are taking turns holding Ethan. Bart is holding him right now. He was hoping to make just one more sunrise with him. Tomorrow, the 4th, Ethan would have been nine months old. He made it pretty close. His heart is still beating. He is a tough little guy. We don't know how long we have with him so we are cherishing every second. We are pretty sad that Andy is sedated and didn't get to say goodbye. He will wake up and not know where his baby brother is.

Once Ethan's heart rate reached zero, the doctor, who was standing next to us watching the numbers slowly fall, came up to us and said, "… and, he's gone." I will never forget those words as long as I live. She turned off the heart monitor so that the beeping sound didn't make the painful reality of his parting any worse than it already was. The nurses told us we could hold Ethan as long as we wanted, and they brought us a little memory kit so we could clip a lock of his hair and put it in a little envelope and make handprint and footprint molds in clay. I took every little piece of Ethan that I could. I took a huge chunk of hair because I knew that I wasn't ever going to get another chance. After we had held him for about fifteen minutes, we knew that nothing more was going to change. There was something very unsatisfying about holding our baby's body when his soul was no longer in it. It was so clear to me that what was left was just a shell; the real Ethan was not there.

After the nurses took Ethan's body away, Bart and I returned to the conference room to tell our family that he was gone. Then Bart went one last time to the computer to thank everyone in cyberspace for staying up all night praying with us and to let them know that they could go to bed.

> *God just took little Ethan home at 4:10 a.m. His mom and I are going to miss him so much. He was the best little baby anyone could ask for. Thank you to all of you for praying so much for Ethan. Please continue to pray for Andy. He is still in ICU.*

With that, we headed back to the Ronald McDonald House to try to get some rest. In the morning we would officially turn all of our concern and prayers in Andy's direction because Ethan no longer needed them. He had been completely healed and was safe and sound in the arms of Jesus. Andy, however, was at a critical point in his recovery. He seemed to have hit a plateau; he was not getting worse, as he had been every day since he arrived, but he had not started to get better, either. We prayed that the next day he would show some signs of improvement.

11

Still Trustworthy?

L ater that same morning, I remember lying next to Bart in the queen-sized bed at the Ronald McDonald House. It was the first time we had actually slept in the same bed since Ethan had been admitted to the hospital, but no matter how hard I tried, I couldn't sleep. It was already after 4:30 a.m. We would need to get up in a few hours anyway. I had this nagging question lurking in the back of my mind, but I dreaded actually saying it out loud. Fortunately, I didn't have to; Bart beat me to it.

He looked at me and asked, "Do you think we should go ahead and plan Ethan's funeral? Or should we wait and see if we'll need to have one for Andy, too?"

I simply sighed and said, "I really don't know. I was going to ask you the same thing."

Looking back now, it seems like such a horrible conversation for any two parents to have. But at the time, that was the reality that we were facing. Neither of us wanted to go through all of the pain of having a funeral for one of our children, only to turn around and have a second one a few days later. At that point we weren't sure if Andy was going to pull through. He was still sedated and on a breathing tube. His lungs weren't clear enough to try to remove the tube, and his lab results weren't exactly encouraging.

Once we got out of bed and returned to the hospital, we faced our most trying day yet. It was very difficult for us to be at the hospital without Ethan. That was the whole reason we had gone there in the first place: to help him get better. Now he was gone, and Andy was hanging on for dear life. In a typical situation in which parents lose a child after an illness or a stay in the hospital, they would return home to a more familiar and comfortable environment to begin the grieving process, surrounded by family and friends. But because Andy was still in the hospital, we had to stay there, almost delaying the grieving process until later when it would really set in that things would never be the same.

After we met with the doctors during their morning rounds, we got a little bit of encouraging news from Andy's lab results, and we began to believe that he just might pull through. As we had hoped, it looked as if the HLH had been stopped before it had done too much damage. Andy would not need chemotherapy. With the help of the antiviral drugs and the immunoglobulin infusions, he would be able to fight the Adenovirus. His liver and kidneys were not as damaged as Ethan's had been, and he would be able to handle the liter of fluid that went along with the anti-viral drug.

The doctors actually learned a lot about how to treat Andy—and how *not* to treat him—from Ethan. Part of the problem with Ethan was that while the chemotherapy did seem to stave off the HLH, it weakened what was left of his immune system—mainly the T-cells—and he was unable to fight off the Adenovirus. Instead, the virus was left unchecked, running rampant throughout his body, overtaking all of his vital organs. Ethan helped the doctors save Andy's life. It was the best gift a brother could give.

Later that day, our pastor from back home came to the hospital to visit. He pulled Bart and me aside and confessed that he was confused by what the Lord had been impressing upon his heart. Over and over, while our pastor was praying for Ethan's healing, the Lord kept asking him the same question: "Do you trust me?" Our pastor assumed that by that God meant, *Hey, of course I'll heal him. I'm God. Don't you trust me?* But when God did not heal Ethan, several people, including ourselves and our pastor, were left with some unanswered questions.

Bart then shared that he had also felt the Lord was asking him the same question. I didn't know it at the time, but Bart told us that the first night he arrived at the hospital, he could not sleep. God had some business to conduct with him and he would not let Bart sleep until it was done. While Bart was praying for Ethan's healing, he felt that God was asking him, "Do you trust me?"

Bart had to admit that at first his answer was: *Yes, I trust you… as long as you heal Ethan.* This must not have been the answer God wanted to hear because Bart was left feeling uneasy until he completely surrendered to the Lord and gave everything over, even little Ethan, and placed him in God's care—no matter what happened. Like our pastor, Bart was also hoping that trusting God with Ethan meant that God would heal him and keep him here on earth with us, but that is not what happened. Now what were we to think?

We were planning to make a quick trip home the next day to make funeral arrangements for Ethan. I didn't really want to go because it meant leaving Andy for an entire day. I figured anything could happen. What if he suddenly took a turn for the worse? But Bart's mother and my mom volunteered to stay with him, so I felt like he was in good hands.

We met with the funeral director and picked out a little oak casket for Ethan that looked like a mini version of an adult casket. I remember thinking how wrong it was that caskets even came that small. We then chose the verses and songs that we wanted at the service. We thought it would be appropriate to sing "He's Got the Whole World in His Hands" at the funeral. It was a song that we played quite often in the car because it was on one of Emma's favorite children's CDs. Andy and Emma would make us sing that song over and over, inserting people's names into the verses. We would sing, "He's got Andy and Emma in his hands, He's got Andy and Emma in his hands…" And then we would sing, "He's got Mommy and Ethan in His hands…" We thought there was no more appropriate song now that God literally had Ethan in his hands. So we chose the verse that said, "He's got the tiny little baby in his hands," to be sung at the funeral. I never thought that a children's Bible song would ever have such deep meaning for me. God did have Ethan in his hands, and even though it didn't seem like it at the time, Ethan was in God's hands even before he went to heaven. Even now I can't listen to that song without thinking of Ethan or his funeral.

We returned to the hospital that night after meeting with the funeral director and had good news from the doctors: Andy's lungs had cleared enough to remove his breathing tube the next morning. I was both relieved and scared at the same time. There was the slight possibility that when the tube came out, Andy wouldn't be able to breathe on his own. That scared me a little bit, but the doctors also said that the longer the tube was left in, the chances of him not being able to breathe unassisted would be greater, so removing the tube seemed like the best option. Besides that, Andy was beginning to grow restless, even under sedation. I was afraid he was going to wake up and pull the tube out of his mouth all by himself!

As planned, in the morning Andy's breathing tube was removed and his lungs took over the job of breathing once again. What a relief. His throat was sore and he couldn't talk much, but he did manage to say the word *no* a few times as I was flipping through the television channels, trying to find something he would like to watch. From the look on his face, it was obvious that even the smallest little word took him a lot of effort and caused him a great deal of pain. But apparently it didn't cause him any pain to swallow because boy, could he eat! He must have been starving after eating only PediaSure via a feeding tube for six days. He ate a big breakfast that morning, and that evening for supper he ate chicken nuggets, macaroni and cheese, and a hot dog. I didn't know his stomach could hold so much food.

Although Andy loved mac and cheese and hot dogs, the look on his face was one of apprehension. I really don't think he knew where he was or why he was there. When he had first arrived at the hospital—as a patient, not a visitor—he was so out of it he probably didn't even recall being admitted. Now he was in a bed with IV lines running into his chest and arm, and he had a killer sore throat. I bet he was pretty scared. Bart and I didn't leave his side for most of the day, and we didn't mind that one bit.

We felt good enough about Andy's condition to go to Ethan's funeral, but we didn't want Andy to be alone because we knew he was scared. We asked Bart's mother if she would mind missing the funeral to stay with Andy. I knew it would be a hard decision for her, and I'll always remember what she said: "I have two grandsons that I love very much, but this one needs me more right now."

With that reassurance, we headed home after supper to prepare for Ethan's funeral, which would be the next morning. It would be the first time I had been home in two weeks.

I managed to make it through the funeral rather well. I was more concerned with the message that was shared during the service than anything else. Would people at the funeral hear the gospel? After all, wasn't that what this was all about, anyway? Didn't God allow Ethan to die for some really big purpose? I secretly hoped that someone would come up to me after the funeral service and tell me that his or her life had been forever changed because of it. If that didn't happen, I was going to be pretty upset.

I kept my emotions under control throughout most of the service. I didn't sing "He's Got the Whole World in His Hands." I just couldn't bring myself to do it. I don't think I cried much until the very end, when Bart, his dad, brother and my stepdad carried the casket down the aisle and out the door. Emma and I followed behind, and without warning, I just lost it. It finally hit me that the casket lid was closed, and it wouldn't be opened again. I would never again see my baby's face, this side of heaven. Soon, he would be laid in the ground and I would really have to say goodbye to him—the most painful goodbye that I have ever said to anyone. For just a few more minutes, he was still here, right in front of me, but not for long. The only word I can use to describe how I felt at that moment is: helpless. I have always been the kind of person who tries to "fix" things when they go wrong. My mind was constantly trying to figure out some way that we could escape this, or undo it; make it go away. But there was nothing. There was no way of changing the fact that Ethan was gone.

Because it was so small, Ethan's casket was loaded into the back of a minivan that belonged to the funeral home. I still thought he deserved a full-sized hearse, but maybe there wasn't one available. I will give the funeral director the benefit of the doubt on that one. Those who joined us at the cemetery all huddled behind us underneath a green canvas canopy, since it was early April and the air was cold and the wind was biting. Our pastor said a few words; then we prayed, and that was it. Ethan's casket wasn't lowered into the ground until after we left.

I was doing a good job of keeping my composure until my brother-in-law hugged me and told me that I was a good mother. He wanted to comfort me, and I really appreciated it, but after all that had happened, I just didn't agree with him. I had failed my little boy in the biggest possible way. What kind of a mother lets her child die when there were obviously warning signs and things that could have been done much earlier to prevent him from ever getting so sick? After the burial, all I wanted to do was get back to the hospital and be with Andy and make sure that I didn't let the same thing happen to him.

Our family Christmas card picture from December
2005. It was one of the only family pictures we had taken
while Ethan was with us.

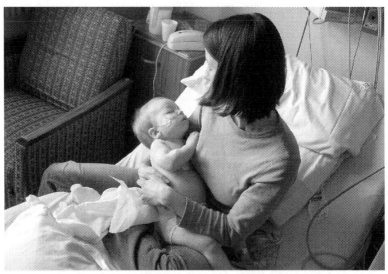

Ethan and Jessica at St. Mary's hospital in Duluth, MN,
waiting to hear the results of Ethan's liver tests.

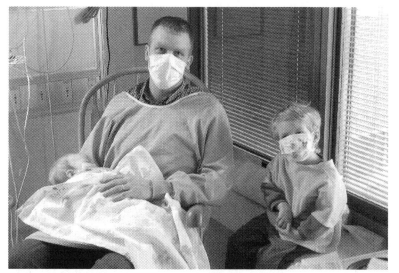

Bart holds Ethan and spends time with Andy, who was
just visiting.

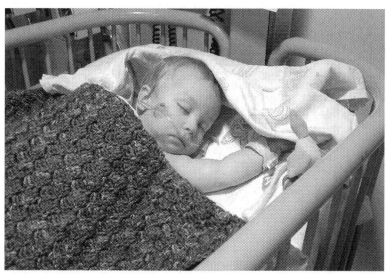

Ethan looked like a little angel, even when he was very
sick.

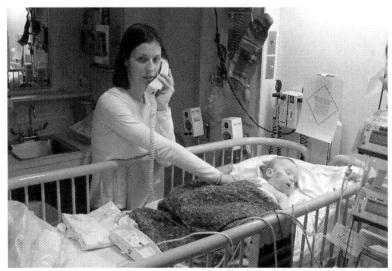

Jessica talks to the doctor back home while putting pressure on Ethan's bleeding Hickman catheter.

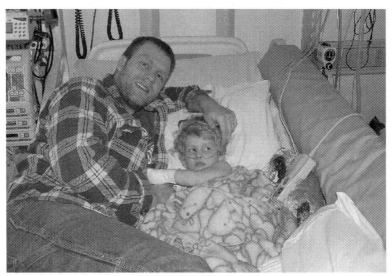

Bart sits with Andy, who doesn't know what to think after waking up in the hospital.

Andy offers moral support to little Mathew during one of
his first subcutaneous IgG injections.

Andy, Jessica, Mathew, Bart and Emma on a trip to
Glacier National Park in August 2007, where no moose
were spotted.

Jessica, Gavin, Andy, Emma, Bart and Mathew in front of the Christmas stockings, where Ethan is always remembered.

The last "new" picture of Ethan, which Jessica received from her aunt several years after Ethan passed away.

12

The New Normal

When we first arrived at the Ronald McDonald House, I heard several people refer to the current stage of their lives as their "new normal." Everyone who was at the Ronald McDonald House was there because in one way or another, their lives had been turned upside-down, and they were living away from home in a strange in-between state of limbo, waiting for a sick child to get better—or not. After Ethan passed away, I really started to hate the term "new normal." Let me tell you what I thought about *my* new normal: I hated it! There was absolutely nothing normal about it! It was just plain wrong. We went from two kids, to three kids, and back to two again. Tell me what is normal about that? It simply goes against nature. Young families are supposed to grow, not get smaller.

Even after Ethan passed away, we were still living in a state of limbo. Andy was still in the hospital, although by that time we knew he would pull through. We longed for the day that we could go home and start living a normal life again, and yet we feared it at the same time because we knew that it would not be normal—not the normal we were used to. Although it may seem strange, being at the hospital made me feel closer to Ethan. It was the last place where he had lived—the last place I saw him. When we went home,

I knew it would be difficult; Ethan was supposed to be there, but he wouldn't be. I felt like once I left the hospital to return home, I would be leaving Ethan for good, and it would finally start to feel real. I didn't know if I could handle that.

Andy ended up staying in the hospital for a few more weeks, although after a little while he was changed to out-patient status. We were still staying in the Ronald McDonald House, but Andy could be there with us and not in a hospital room. We would go into the hospital every day to have his IV lines flushed and have blood work done. Andy would also receive his anti-viral medication via an IV, along with the necessary extra fluid. When he wasn't in the hospital, we had to occupy ourselves in Minneapolis or watch a movie in our room at the Ronald McDonald House.

Once the doctors were certain that the virus was mostly gone, and that Andy wouldn't have any kind of relapse, we were told we could finally go home. But first, we had to be trained to flush Andy's central line and change the dressing, since he would be living with it for a few months until there was no longer a possibility that he would need it. After we felt comfortable flushing the lines with Heparin and pulling the sticky dressing off *without* pulling the tubes right out of Andy's chest, we loaded up all of the stuff we had accumulated over the past month and headed home.

The one thing I kept telling the doctors was that I wanted Andy to be home by his third birthday—and he was. He made it home a few days before. On his birthday we had a big celebration. Normally I don't like having big gatherings at my house, but this time there was a reason to make an exception. We invited about thirty of our close friends and relatives and some of Bart's coworkers over to our house for Andy's birthday. But this wasn't just a birthday party; it was a celebration of life. And while we were extremely happy and grateful to have Andy back home with us, there was always that feeling that it could be so much better…if Ethan were home with us, too. It was bittersweet.

After the excitement of having Andy back home started to die down, I realized that life kept marching on—whether I was ready to join in the parade or not—so I went back to doing what I had done before this horrible ordeal ever happened: "normal" stuff. As silly as it may seem, one of the hardest things for me to do when I got home was Ethan's laundry. Because I had left for the hospital in such a hurry, I had several loads of dirty clothes that needed to be washed, and of course, some of those clothes were Ethan's. But now that he was gone, this once mundane, everyday chore suddenly took on super-sentimental meaning. I even wondered, *Should I do his laundry now, and forever put an end to washing Ethan's clothes? Or should I keep them in the laundry basket for just a little while longer? At least then I will still have his clothes in the basket with everyone else's clothes.*

In the end, I decided to go ahead and do the laundry—every load of it. If I had put it off, it would have been like pretending, for just a moment, that maybe all of this was just a bad dream. Maybe if I still had baby laundry to wash, then I still had a baby. But I didn't. Part of me knew that it was healthier just to dive right in and get it over with than it would be to put it off for too long, delaying the inevitable.

I turned doing Ethan's last laundry into a ceremony of sorts. I carefully separated his clothes by color, carefully taking in the feel and scent of each piece of clothing, and then added the clothes to the other laundry. By the end of the day, I had washed it all. When his clothes were dry, I folded them and made a little pile just for his clothes, the same as I always had. I took them up to his room and put the clothes away in the dresser or in the closet, just as I would have on any normal laundry day. But there was one difference: Ethan would not be dirtying any more clothes for me to wash ever again. I would never have this chance again. So for this last time, I did everything very slowly and reveled in every second of it.

Soon after returning home from the hospital, I began to take a ride on a wild emotional roller coaster. There were times when I would be talking on the phone to a friend who had called to comfort me, and by the end of the conversation, I would find myself comforting *her* instead. I could go from crying to laughing in a single sentence.

Sometimes I would be downright elated in the midst of my intense grief. In these moments I felt like I was on some sort of spiritual mountaintop, and I wanted to preach to anyone who would listen the message of how God had chosen to use my little boy as a way to bring others closer to him. God had used the short life of Ethan Johnson to show people what was truly important in life. What an honor that Ethan was chosen out of all of the little babies in the world for such an important task! I remember saying more than once, "Ethan may have touched more people in his nine months of life than some people will touch in ninety years!"

Unfortunately, these emotional highs did not last long. Most of the time, I felt like everything in life was meaningless. I could honestly say I could relate to Solomon in the book of Ecclesiastes: everything was meaningless.[3] Life without Ethan was meaningless. If I didn't have two other kids to take care of, I could have stayed in bed all day. Why get up? There were only meaningless chores to be done. What was the point of doing laundry now that Ethan's laundry was done, and I would only have to wash clothes for four people instead of five? Why cook supper? I didn't feel like eating anyway.

I used to be a rather materialistic person; name brands meant a lot to me. Having nice things and a nice house and a newer car made me happy. But after Ethan died, I would have traded everything I owned to have him back. I would have lived in a cardboard box, worn plastic bags instead of clothes, and driven a car that was so rusty you could see through it if only he were there with me.

I no longer found joy in the things I once loved doing. I couldn't read the books I used to enjoy. What was the point? They were only meant for entertainment, and I certainly didn't feel like being entertained—how petty. I couldn't watch television, either. What a waste of time! Even my favorite shows and movies no longer appealed to me.

I thought back to the time when we first moved back to Minnesota and recalled feeling very alone because I had left several friends in Iowa only to come to a town where I didn't have any close friends. Now I thought, *Who cares about friends! I could have a hundred friends here and I would trade them all to have Ethan back.*

When I look back now, I can see that God was using the loss of Ethan in my life to put me through a sort of refining process. It was as if I were a piece of wood, and he was whittling away at my imperfections. He was removing all of my rotten pieces, all of my extra branches and worm holes. He would keep pruning me until all that was left was my raw, inner person, with none of the baggage that had accumulated over the years.

As strange as it may sound, this process actually felt more freeing than painful. I felt like finally my priorities were more in line with God's. I realized what really mattered in life—and what didn't. How much time had I wasted over the years worrying about things that really didn't matter in the big picture? I promised myself I would not forget the lessons that I learned going through this process of losing Ethan. It would never again take a tragedy like this to get my attention—at least, it better not. It was just way too painful, and if it happened again, I didn't think I'd be able to survive it.

13

Denial, I Didn't Recognize You!

Denial: an unconscious thought process whereby one allays anxiety by refusing to acknowledge the existence of certain unpleasant aspects of external reality or of one's thoughts, feelings, etc.: now often in the phrase **in denial.**

If you would have asked me after Ethan's death whether or not I was in denial, my answer would have been easy: no way! Denial was for delusional people—people who were already bordering on insanity before experiencing the loss that inevitably pushed them over the edge into...*denial*. That did not describe me. I was under no illusion that things were still the same as they were before. I knew for a fact that my son was gone. I couldn't argue with the evidence all around me which clearly pointed to the fact that there was someone very important missing in our house. At nighttime, the silence coming from his bedroom was so loud, it was almost deafening, shouting out in the darkness, "Ethan is not here!"

For four and a half years, up until Ethan passed away, we had grown accustomed to life with a baby in the house. As soon as one baby was approaching the age of two, we would have another one. I was used to getting up at least once every night to tend to some crying child, whether infant or toddler, and my body was almost trained to wake up at certain points throughout the night. Now with Ethan gone, I was being given the chance to sleep through the night, even though I didn't want to, and I couldn't sleep at all. Everything around me screamed the fact that Ethan was not there anymore. All day and all night I was reminded of that fact, and I wasn't trying to pretend that he was there. Clearly, I was not in denial.

I wasn't going around setting a plate in front of Ethan's high chair at meal time or laying out clothes for him to wear every day. I took his car seat out of our Suburban after a few days because seeing it there, empty, was more than I could handle. I knew he was gone, and there was no use fighting that fact. Little did I know that I was actually *in denial* about being in denial because there was one thing I *was* refusing to accept: the fact that my new Ethan-less existence was permanent—not just temporary.

One of the only things that got me through my next breath in the early days after losing Ethan, although completely unintentional, was to become obsessed with heaven and the rapture.[4] I figured that there was absolutely no way God expected me to live much longer with the grief I was experiencing, so surely the rapture was imminent. Ethan's death was to be the monumental event that would usher in the end times. Forget the rebuilding of the temple or the Jews returning to their homeland; Ethan Johnson had died and that meant that Jesus was returning at any moment. He just had to be. God was going to do something big through this.

I went off the deep end a little and read every book I could get my hands on about heaven, the rapture, and end times prophecy. I began checking the television news headlines first thing every morning for news of the formation of a ten-nation confederacy or the signing of some kind of peace treaty in Israel. And actually, there was a lot in the news about Israel in 2006, but eventually, things quieted down. That was very disappointing.

I was quite content with the fact that I was a short-timer here on earth. This way of thinking actually benefitted me because not only did I not *want* to do my housewife duties (because they were meaningless), now I no longer *needed* to do them. Why bother doing laundry? Why should I go grocery shopping? After all, we're only going to be here a few more days, and then Jesus is going to come and take us to heaven. I'll be reunited with Ethan in the sky, and then I will get a new body, so there's no need to stock the freezer.

I even considered writing letters to our distant relatives or neighbors who might possibly be left behind after the rapture. I figured that after hearing the news of massive numbers of people mysteriously disappearing in an instant, they would try to call us to see if we were okay. After several days of not hearing from us, they would surely come to our house to look for us. They would enter our house—which would be unlocked, since we left without warning—and look through our stuff, hoping to find clues that would lead them to the cause of our disappearance. They would find Bibles placed randomly throughout the house with passages about the rapture highlighted and marked with post-it notes. Then they would find the envelopes that I also strategically placed all over the house containing letters reassuring them of our safety:

> *Don't worry about us. We are okay. We went to heaven. Read the passages I have marked in the Bible to find out how you can go there, too. And please help yourselves to any of our frozen food or canned goods; I would not want them to go to waste.*

I had it all planned out. But after several months went by and the rapture did *not* occur (if it did, I missed it), I resigned myself to the fact that I had no choice but to keep living here on earth. As much as it pained me to accept it, I might be around for a while.

I guess my obsession with the rapture was a way for me to avoid dealing with the reality that Ethan was gone, and that I may have to live fifty more years without him. Once I realized that, it was like the wound that Ethan's death had left in my heart had been reopened, and I had to deal with it all over again. I had already delayed my grieving process by being in the hospital with Andy after Ethan's death. Then I put it off by denying that we would be separated for long. I had temporarily delayed asking the hard questions by pretending I didn't need to because it wouldn't matter; I was on my way to heaven. But eventually, I had to face the facts, and it was hard.

How would I be able to go on without my baby? If I really wasn't going to see him *in a few days*, how would I get through the rest of my life? The only reason I got out of bed each day was because I still had two kids on earth who needed me, and I should have been thankful for that. But for some reason, the two kids on earth still couldn't compete for my attention which was devoted almost completely to the one little child who was in heaven. I wanted him back, and if I couldn't have him back, then I would go to where he was. The rapture was my only escape.

Unfortunately, every day the sun rose and set. I was still here, and Ethan was still gone. If only there were a phone line that connected heaven and earth, so I could at least talk to him. Or maybe something like Skype would be better since Ethan hadn't even said his first word yet before he left, and I didn't want to miss that. I just needed something more than what I had, which was nothing. I decided that since none of this was possible, I would just talk to God, and tell him little messages to give Ethan when he had the chance. "Tell Ethan I love him. Tell him I miss him. Please tell Ethan not to forget me and to wait for me; I'll get there as soon as I can."

One good thing did come out of my obsession with heaven: I learned a lot about my future home. I wanted to know everything there was to know about the place where my son was now living. I had so many questions: What does Ethan look like in heaven? How old is he? Is he going to stay a baby until I get there, or will he grow at the same rate he would have on earth? Or maybe he'll instantly transform into a thirty-year-old. Will he remember me? Is he with his grandpa who he never got to meet on earth? Or is some stranger who never had a child on earth living out her unfulfilled dreams by raising *my* son in heaven instead of me?

The sad thing is that I should have already been curious about heaven. It is, after all, the place where I will live for all eternity. Why would it take losing a child to finally start me thinking about heaven? Jesus has been there all this time, preparing a place for me that is beyond anything I could ever imagine, and for some reason I was more *afraid* to know what it was like than I was curious. I almost assumed I would be bored there, like my life would end after I died and went to heaven.

After all of my heavenly research, I discovered what every Christian should already know: our lives will only just begin when we get to heaven. We are living in a world that has been tainted by the curse of sin, and yet, we are so used to it that we're afraid to leave it. Why is that?

I know, just as he promised he would, God has made many good things come from our tragedy. But if I could name one good thing that has come from it, it would be the fact that I finally have my eyes set on eternity—on things above, not things on earth. I am ashamed and embarrassed to admit that knowing Jesus personally wasn't enough to set my sights on eternal things. It took losing my son to cause me to feel a real connection to my heavenly home. I don't know why it has to be so hard, but I can now say I am excited to go to heaven. I no longer fear death (at least not my own). One thing I *do* know about the rapture is this: the Bible says it is imminent. It was imminent five years ago, so now it is even more imminent than it was then. If you want your friends and relatives in heaven with you, please don't wait and try to tell them about God's plan for salvation after the rapture by leaving sticky notes in your Bible—tell them now.

14

Here Come the Hard Questions

Once I finally admitted to myself that I really might have to live without Ethan, the hard questions came crashing down on me like an avalanche. Suddenly, I was inundated with uncertainties and self-doubt. I found myself constantly playing the *What If* game. Believe me, that is one game you don't want to play; you will never win. Even so, I couldn't help but ask, *What if?* from time to time. There were so many different scenarios running through my mind all the time, and at the end of each one, Ethan would have lived ... *if only.*

Of course, looking at the situation in retrospect, everything made perfect sense. I had told myself all along that it wasn't normal for a kid to be sick as often as Andy was. I should have trusted my gut instincts at the time—if only I knew then what I know now. Maybe I could have done something differently. Maybe if I would have been more aggressive with the doctors in Iowa when Andy first started to get sick all the time and asked them to test his immune system, they would have discovered that he had no B-cells. He could have begun treatment so much sooner. Then when Ethan was born, he would have been tested for the disease right away, and he would still be here.

And then there was that unrelenting question, *Why?* No matter how many times I tried to comfort myself with the traditional, old stand-by answers like, "God's ways are mysterious," or, "It was simply God's will," that just wasn't enough to satisfy my curiosity. I felt God owed me an explanation. Maybe if I at least knew why God had allowed Ethan to die, then I could go on and live the rest of my life in peace while I waited to get to heaven and be with Ethan again.

Sometimes I wondered if it was my fault that Ethan had died. Was it because I had been distant from the Lord for so long? Was God trying to get my attention and I was just so hard-headed that it took the loss of a child to bring me back to him?

Maybe it was simply a lack of faith on my part. Did I not pray hard enough when Ethan was sick? Did I not pray in the right way? Maybe by using the phrase *if it is your will* at the end of my prayers, it was like giving God some sort of escape clause—like he didn't have to answer my prayer if it wasn't his will. Maybe I should have simply demanded that God heal Ethan, and if it wasn't his will, then he would just have to change his will...or else.

Probing into the mysterious ways of God did not answer any of my questions, but instead, caused deeper questions to pop up. It seems that any time a person experiences some form of terrible loss, it is only a matter of time before he or she ends up referring back to the life of Job—the master of trials—for some sort of insight into the behind-the-scenes workings of God. My study of Job may have started out as a quest for comfort and answers, but it only ended up leading to further questions, which in turn led to more and more questions about the exact cause of Ethan's death.

Some of the questions I asked myself on an almost daily basis were: *Did God do this? Did he take Ethan because it was simply his will? Was Ethan's death necessary to bring about some greater good? Or did Satan do it, just to be mean?* Or to complicate things even further: *Did Satan ask God if he could take Ethan, and God, like in the book of Job, simply gave him permission?*

Some of the books I received after Ethan died suggested a completely different approach to prayer and healing which left me thoroughly confused. After reading one book, I wondered, *Did Satan take Ethan and God was powerless to do anything about it, and the only thing that could have prevented it was the prayers of God's people? If so, what was wrong with the thousands of prayers being sent up to heaven on Ethan's behalf during his almost two-week-long battle with HLH?*

The questions were unending, and it seemed there was no way to escape them.

15

Why Pray?

I may have had a spiritual reawakening after Ethan's death, but two areas that did not grow in a positive direction were my prayer life and my trust in God. Sure, I knew more about heaven now. I was finally being used in a ministry role again, writing monthly articles for our church newsletter, trying to encourage others with the spiritual truths that God was teaching me through the circumstances in my life at the time. My priorities were more on track than they had ever been, and I had gone through a refining process. But all of this had come about because my worst fear had come true: I had lost one of my children. God had taken away my baby, even though we prayed that he wouldn't. So where did that leave my relationship with God? On pretty shaky ground, to say the least.

Two months after Ethan passed away, I mustered up as much of my wounded faith as I could, and I took another chance at trusting God—this time with the health of a new baby.

Bart and I had always talked about having four kids. When Ethan first passed away, we considered counting our blessings, being thankful that Andy hadn't died, and stopping there. But something inside me kept telling me not to let death or disease have the final say in how many children we had. I knew I wanted more kids, and so did Bart; although we were a little apprehensive, knowing that the chance of having another child with XLA was one in four. I really wanted another boy—one who could wear Ethan's clothes and sleep in his room and play with his toys. Unfortunately, having a boy would increase the chance of the disease occurring from twenty-five to fifty percent. But it was still okay with me. I could justify taking care of another child with XLA because if Ethan had lived, which is what I would have wanted, then I would have taken care of him and cherished every second of it.

Things had already gotten a little easier with the introduction of subcutaneous immunoglobulin injections, which I had begun doing at home after Andy's Hickman catheter was removed. Although these injections had to be done weekly, rather than monthly, it was much easier than going to a clinic for a four-hour-long intravenous infusion. I had gotten the hang of connecting the syringe to the tubing, drawing up the medicine, priming the pump and sticking the needle into the fatty sections of my son's skin. I did it every week for Andy; I would have done it for Ethan, and if the new baby was a boy and also had XLA, then I would do it for him, too.

There was still the chance that if I had another boy, he could be completely healthy—and that's what I was praying for. We had already had two boys with the disease, even though the chances were one out of every four births, so we had already more than met our quota. I prayed every day of my pregnancy that if the baby was a boy, then he would be healthy. I prayed that if he had the genetic defect already, then God would heal him from inside the womb. I knew that God could do that. I actually had faith for the first time since Ethan died that my prayers would be answered.

God even gave me a little clue that the baby would be a boy: he gave him a name. After using the only two boy names that I liked—or that Bart and I could agree on—we couldn't come up with a third. I always liked names that sounded old-fashioned, or English in origin. Bart seemed to gravitate toward Viking names, like Sven or Erik. I could just hear him saying, "Axel is a nice name." We had only a few weeks until our baby would be born, and if it was a boy he would have no name. One day I was standing in front of our refrigerator and staring at the pictures of our three children, which were held up by shiny plastic magnets cut out in the shape of the letters of their names: Emma, Andrew, and Ethan. Each of our kids' first or middle names was a family name, and I thought to myself how nice it would be if this next child could somehow be named after the three other kids.

I looked at the letters in each of the kids' names, mentally moving them around in my head, and tried to come up with a new name that used at least two letters from each name. What I came up with was: Mathew. Only, it was spelled with one *t*, not two like the traditional spelling. I wondered, *Is that even a name? Has anyone ever spelled "Mathew" that way before?* Not even two seconds had passed after the question entered my mind when I felt the Lord prompting me to look at a wedding invitation that had come in the mail the day before. It was for one of Bart's engineering students. I took the invitation out of the envelope and looked at it. The student's middle name was Mathew—with one *t*! I had my answer: Mathew was a real name, and it had been used before!

After that I began to see one-*t* Mathews everywhere: on the credits at the end of movies, in magazines, on baseball caps with company logos embroidered across the front, and other places where I least expected to see the name. I felt like the Lord had named this child; he would be a boy, and his name would be Mathew. It seemed like God was going out of his way to say, "Yes, he will be a boy, and he will NOT have XLA." I felt at peace about this new life growing inside me; he would be fine. (And if the baby had been a girl after all that, I would have been seriously confused.)

And so, only a week before the one-year anniversary of Ethan's death, little Mathew—with one *t*—was born. We had his cord blood shipped off to a lab in Washington to be tested for XLA. The results would take several weeks, but I knew in my heart that he would be okay. After all, why would God have made Mathew a boy, and go to all of the trouble of naming him for us, if he was going to have this disease as well? I also later found out that Mathew (or Matthew) meant "Gift of God." God had given us a gift: a healthy baby boy. Besides, Bart and I already had enough on our plates, so to speak. We were just learning how to take care of a child with a serious disease—the same disease that had claimed the life of our other little boy—so God surely understood that giving us a healthy baby would be the nicest thing to do.

When Mathew was about three weeks old, I got a phone call. I had been getting butterflies in my stomach every time the phone rang since he was born, knowing that one of those times it would be the doctor calling with the test results. I don't know why I was so nervous since I knew what the results would be, but still, I jumped every time. Now it was actually happening.

I answered the phone and heard Dr. Kumar say, "Jessica. How are you." It wasn't a question; it was more of a statement. I wasn't exactly encouraged by the tone of his voice.

"Fine," I replied, waiting for what he would say next.

"I'm afraid I have some bad news." That was it. My heart sank into the pit of my stomach; I felt the blood drain from my face, and a feeling like nervousness filled my whole body. I looked over at Bart, who by that time had figured out who was on the other end of the line. Tears welled up in my eyes, but I did my best to keep my composure—at least while I was on the phone.

"I don't understand," I said. "We've already had two kids with XLA. I thought the odds were one in four."

"Yes, but that means one in four each time you have a child. With every new pregnancy the odds start over; they're not cumulative."

I wished they were. Then "the odds" would know that we already had enough boys with XLA, and they could go knocking on someone else's door. But it was too late to change anything now, and we felt that we at least knew what to expect from the disease, having cared for Andy for almost a year with no huge setbacks.

Mathew continued to grow into a beautiful little boy, and since he had the benefit of being diagnosed with XLA at birth, he began receiving his IgG injections at the age of six weeks and was able to stay relatively healthy. Life had begun to seem somewhat *normal* again, and it felt really good to have a baby in the house once more.

But because of what I considered to be yet another "defeat" in the prayer arena, I felt a dark shadow lingering somewhere in my soul every time I tried to pray. I began to wonder if God even listened to my prayers—if he even cared. If his will was set in stone, and he already knew the way things were going to turn out, then what was the point of praying? I had prayed for Ethan to live, but he didn't. I prayed that Mathew would not have XLA, but he did.

My desire to pray grew smaller and smaller. I began intentionally making myself busy at bedtime when Bart would pray with the kids in their rooms. I just didn't feel like going through the motions when my heart wasn't in it. Instead of praying, I would think, *Why bother? God will just do what he wants anyway.*

My attitude toward prayer had definitely become a cynical one. On one particular Sunday morning at church, an older friend of mine got up during our sharing time and told the story of how God had protected her daughter during a terrible car accident. The car was smashed in the front, back, and passenger side. The only place that was left somewhat intact was the driver's seat where she had been sitting. Everyone in the congregation could be heard whispering, "Praise the Lord. Thank you, Jesus." I was not among those whispering praises. Instead, I was sitting quietly in my seat, asking God, *Why would you so obviously protect that girl when her mother had absolutely no idea she was even in danger that day, and was probably not even aware that she should be praying for her safety, and yet when Ethan was sick and everyone was praying for him, you just turned a deaf ear?*

It wasn't that I wasn't glad the girl was all right. I cared about her and her family and would have been devastated for them if anything would have happened. But this wasn't the first time that an event like this had happened, and God received all the credit and all the glory for his wonderful provision. I couldn't help but wonder what people would be saying if things had turned out differently. Would they still be praising Jesus? I was becoming more and more confused. It seemed to me that there was just no rhyme or reason when it came to prayer; instead it was all very haphazard. Sometimes it worked and sometimes it didn't. When it worked, God would be praised. But when it didn't, then what? How was I supposed to feel when my prayers seemed to go unanswered?

In August 2007, our family took a trip out west to visit Yellowstone and Glacier National Parks. Bart had always loved the mountains and hadn't been to Montana or Wyoming since he was a kid. I had never been that far west, so we decided it was time to take a vacation. Ever since moving to northern Minnesota, it had become sort of a dream of mine to see a real, live moose, since there were no moose in Ohio, where I grew up. Even after three years of living in Minnesota, I hadn't seen a single one of these seemingly mythical creatures, so I figured going out to Montana and Wyoming would increase my chances. I even prayed about it, trying to increase the likelihood that I would see one. Even as we pulled out of the driveway of our home, ready to trek across four states, I started to believe that God just might grant my small request. It wasn't as if I were asking a lot from him—nothing that would alter the course of history or anything. I just wanted to see a moose. That's all.

After seven days of traveling all the way from Minnesota, through North and South Dakota, Montana, Wyoming, and back to Minnesota, I still hadn't seen one single moose. I saw a thousand buffalo, two grizzly bears and three mountain goats, but no moose. *Why, God? Would it really have been that difficult to just make a moose walk next to the road as we were driving by? I'm sure they were out there somewhere.*

After this most recent disappointment, I had reached a pivotal point in my faith. It may seem silly that something as trivial as not seeing a moose on a trip would cause a crisis of faith, but to me, it was the last straw. I could try and defend God for not answering my moose prayer by saying, "Maybe God just isn't concerned about the *little* things in our lives." But then what about Ethan? That was no trite request; that was a big deal! Maybe God just had his reasons. Maybe Ethan's death really was necessary to complete some part of the bigger picture that we just couldn't see. I'll go along with that. But for something as small and insignificant as seeing a moose while on vacation, couldn't he have bent the rules a little? I'm sure God knew that it meant a lot to me, and that it really would have bolstered my faith at a time when it was in serious trouble. Why couldn't he have just said, "Okay"? Was it too much to ask? Did he even care about me at all?

16

Definitely *Not* Mae Elisabeth

When Mathew was a little over a year old and seemed to be handling his XLA very well, Bart and I decided to have one more child. Like I said before, we had always talked about having four kids, and with Ethan in heaven, it was like we could have a bonus child. It would really be our fifth, but we would only have the stress and chaos of a houseful of four kids. I found out I was pregnant in the fall of 2008. Our due date was at the end of May, but of course, I knew I would be somewhat overdue as usual.

Since Mathew had XLA, despite my prayers to the contrary, I decided that I would start praying even *harder* that this baby was either a girl, or a boy *without* XLA. Even though I was still struggling with the whole issue of prayer, I felt like the Lord had really laid it on my heart that if I prayed this time, everything would turn out fine. Somewhere during my pregnancy with Mathew, I must have done something wrong since I also prayed for him, but he still had XLA. Maybe I had a momentary lapse in faith or something. But that wouldn't happen this time. I prayed before I was pregnant. I prayed during my pregnancy, "Please Lord, let this be a girl so that we don't have to deal with XLA. But if it is your will that we have another boy, please don't let him have XLA. If he already does, I believe you can heal him inside my body. Please Lord, if he already has the genetic defect, please heal him; I know you can." I was very specific, making sure I covered every possible scenario and outcome. I prayed over and over throughout my pregnancy.

I felt the Lord nudging me toward being anointed during the next healing service that we were going to have at church. I went forward and had the elders pray over me and the baby and anoint me with oil. Normally, I would be way too self-conscious to go forward for healing, but the Lord was working on my heart. I believed that this baby would be okay as long as I was obedient, and I did *not* want to mess things up this time.

I wanted to find out ahead of time whether the baby was a boy or a girl, just so that I could prepare my heart. I had saved a girl's name for every baby after Emma: Mae Elisabeth. And every baby after Emma was a boy, so I never got to use it. This was my last chance to have Mae Elisabeth. I always thought she would be part of our family someday. I even talked about her in the future-tense, saying things like, "When Mae Elisabeth is born, she and Emma will share a room," or, "I'm saving Emma's clothes for Mae Elisabeth."

Emma really wanted a sister, too. If this baby was another boy, I figured I would need some time to adjust to the idea and grieve for Mae Elisabeth *before* the birth. I wanted to be completely happy when the baby was born. Bart, as usual, did *not* want to know the gender of the baby; he liked surprises.

He would ask, "Why do you want to know now? So you can worry for the next four months if it's a boy?"

"No," I would answer. "I just want to get Mae Elisabeth out of my mind if it's a boy. And if it's a girl, then I can relax and put XLA out of my mind."

When I was twenty weeks along, we went for our first ultrasound. My obstetrician had some trouble getting the baby to cooperate. His/her legs were tightly closed, with the umbilical cord between them, so the tell-tale parts were hidden from view. My doctor tried several different angles to try to get a good look, but she really couldn't.

"Do you want me to make my best guess?" she asked me.

"Yes," I replied.

The doctor waited until Bart turned his head so he couldn't see her face, and she mouthed the word *girl*.

Unfortunately for Bart, who still wanted to be surprised, the big-eyed, smiley expression on my face gave away the answer. I couldn't help it! I was too excited.

The doctor ordered a follow-up ultrasound with an X-ray technician just to make sure her initial guess was correct.

When we got in the car after that first ultrasound, Bart said, "It's a girl, isn't it?"

"I'm not saying anything," I replied. I just sat quietly in the car, feeling so relieved that for once, I wouldn't have to worry about this disease that had cast a shadow over our lives for the last four years. After feeling like I was unable to have a healthy child, besides Emma, of course, I felt as if a weight had been lifted. I could finally relax and enjoy the rest of my pregnancy, not worrying about test results or diagnoses. I was just a normal person, carrying a normal baby, just like I thought I was during my first three pregnancies—when I was blissfully ignorant of the dangers hidden in my DNA.

For the second ultrasound, which was two weeks later, I went alone. I figured it was pointless for Bart to be there, since we already knew it was most likely a girl. I lay down on the table and cheerfully told the X-ray technician that the baby was a girl, and that I was simply having a second ultrasound to make my obstetrician happy.

The technician looked at the screen, wrinkled her nose and said, "Hmm. If I had to guess, I would say it was a boy. To me, this looks like a...*you know what*."

"Really?" I felt like I had been kicked in the stomach, but I donned my best fake smile and tried to sound excited.

"But," the X-ray technician continued, "I could be wrong."

And in those last four words my hope resided. I had nothing at all against baby boys; I loved them. But given our medical history, and our wonderful track record of not beating the one-in-four odds, I was a little disappointed to hear that this was another boy. I thought that maybe there was still a chance that the X-ray technician was wrong. When I got home, I went to the computer and googled "baby ultrasound mistakes," trying to find ultrasound pictures of baby girls who looked like baby boys. There were tons of them! Unfortunately, most of those pictures had been taken before eighteen weeks gestation. At this point, I was already almost twenty-three weeks along.

"Maybe our baby is just developing slowly," I told Bart. "Or maybe my dates are way off and I'm really not as far along as I thought I was. That has happened before."

Bart told me to get off the internet. I was only torturing myself.

When my obstetrician found out the results from the second ultrasound, she had me come back in and she did a third ultrasound in her office just to make sure. After she had the baby in view, she zoomed in on a very obvious baby boy part and said, "Yep. It's a boy." She clicked a button and printed off a little picture for me, showing the baby boy part, a little arrow pointing to it, and the word *boy* typed next to the arrow. Just in case there was any doubt.

Once I got home, I took out the tubs of seven years' worth of Emma's clothes that I had saved for her little sister and got them ready for a garage sale. There was no use prolonging the inevitable.

Now I would be able to begin getting excited for our new baby boy—our *fourth* baby boy. What on earth would we name him? We had already used three boy names, and God had to give us the third one because we couldn't come up with anything on our own.

About two days before I had the baby, I went to the store with Mathew to get a baby book. (Yes, with the fifth child I was doing things at the last minute.) While I was looking through the baby books, Mathew had gotten interested in the rotating display of plastic mugs with colorful rubber names on them. I hardly even noticed that he had removed two of them from their hooks until he walked over to me, holding two mugs: one pink, and one red.

"Oh, what mugs have you picked out?" I asked.

He held them out in front of me to examine more closely. The pink one said *Jenna.*

"Well, we won't be needing that one," I said, setting it down on the floor. "Let's see this red one."

Mathew handed me the red mug. The name on it was *Gavin*. Somehow it just had this ring to it, even though I had heard it before and dismissed it. Now I felt that Gavin was the perfect name for our little baby boy; it went perfectly with the middle name we had already chosen. I went home and told Bart that it sounded like a cowboy name, hoping that would make the name more appealing to him. It worked! Two days later, our son Gavin was born.

Just as before, we had his cord blood sent off to the lab in Washington, and I waited for that dreaded phone call—only this time it would be good news. I had gone forward for healing, and I had prayed with *much* more faith than the last time. Gavin would be fine.

Finally, the phone call came. Once again it was Dr. Kumar who delivered the news. If I thought he was a little blunt and to-the-point the first time, he was even less interested in small talk this time.

"Jessica." There was a pause while he exhaled deeply. "He has it."

WHAT? I was absolutely baffled. "Are you serious?" I asked. "How can this keep happening?" I felt like we were eligible for entrance into *The Guinness Book of World Records* under the category, "Most occurrences of a genetic disease in a single family." It was almost unbelievable.

I didn't stay on the phone long; there was no point. Dr. Kumar was the last person I was going to have a spiritual conversation with about the will of God, or why bad things happened to good people. Besides, there was nothing more to talk about. I knew the drill; I knew what to expect. The nurse from the specialty pharmacy company would come to my house in a few weeks and train me to give subcutaneous injections to Gavin, even though I knew how to do them already. And that would be it. Gavin would get injections once a week for the rest of his life, and we would take him, along with his two brothers, to the hospital in Minneapolis twice a year for follow-up visits with the hematologists. I would freak out every time he coughed or every time I heard that "something" was going around the school or at church, and I would check the temperature of his forehead with my hand at least seventy times a day—just like with the other two.

By the time Gavin was six weeks old, he was receiving immunoglobulin injections just like Andy and Mathew. But it wasn't so much the fact that Gavin had the disease, or that I had to do injections on three kids now. It was *why*—or maybe even *how*. How could God let this happen, even though I prayed? I trusted him. I believed that Gavin would be okay. I gave everything over to God this time. I had no reservations. No doubts. So what did I do wrong now? I was beginning to feel like I had a huge red target on my back, and I was getting knocked down over and over again. As soon as I tried to get back on my feet again, another blow would come, and I'd be flat on my face. I started to become very discouraged and asked God on more than one occasion, "Can't I catch a break?" It was actually more of a rhetorical question than anything else, because after everything that had happened, I never really expected an answer.

17

Waiting for the Other
Shoe to Drop

From the time that Andy was first diagnosed with an immune deficiency disease, I felt like I was living my life in constant fear of the unknown. I wondered what other dangers may be lurking inside his body, just waiting to be discovered. Was I only fooling myself, thinking that we had a handle on what our life would be like living with this disease? Were the doctors holding back some sort of bad news, waiting until they thought we were ready to handle more? What did they know that we didn't?

The fear only multiplied when Mathew and Gavin were born with the same disease. I lived from doctor's appointment to doctor's appointment, holding my breath while we waited for test results, and breathing a sigh of relief when we walked out the door without hearing that one of the boys had a terminal case of *goodness knows what*. It wouldn't be long before that temporary peace would be replaced by the old familiar fear, which would continue building until the next check-up, or blood test, or chest X-ray.

In February 2010, the boys were due for their bi-annual check-ups with the hematologist in Minneapolis. While we were in the doctor's office, I asked him about Andy's chronic cough, which he had had ever since coming home from the hospital after his bout with pneumonia in 2006. At first it was diagnosed as chronic sinusitis—something that is common in people with immune deficiencies. Over the years, the cough seemed to be getting worse. At first, Andy was put on prophylactic antibiotics to try to keep the sinusitis under control. But now after four years, the antibiotics didn't seem to be working. While we were at our appointment, we had the doctor listen to Andy's lungs, just to make sure we weren't missing something. The hematologist held a stethoscope to Andy's chest as he took several deep breaths. I, on the other hand, *held* my breath while the doctor furrowed his brow and handed the stethoscope to a medical student who was with him. Concern filled the student's expression as well.

"What do you hear?" the hematologist asked the med student.

"Well…there is a slight crackle," the med student replied, still holding the stethoscope to Andy's back.

CLUNK!

What was that? Oh, I think the other shoe just dropped.

As I watched the two doctors exchanging knowing glances, I felt like waving my hand and saying, "Hello? I'm over here. Would you care to inform me about what it is you hear in my son's lungs?" But instead, I just asked, "What do you mean, crackle? Is it pneumonia again?"

"Could be. Let's do a chest X-ray and see if we can get a better look at what's going on."

After the chest X-ray revealed a dark, shaded area in Andy's lower left lobe—the same place where it was shaded when he had pneumonia—the doctor suggested that we make an appointment with the pediatric pulmonary specialist. Of course, we would have to wait several weeks to get an appointment to see him, and until then, all I could do was worry about what he would say.

When the appointment with the pulmonologist finally arrived, we drove down to Minneapolis once again—this time with only Andy. There was no sense in taking the entire crew to his doctor's appointment since we were usually stuck in a tiny examining room for several hours. Andy was scheduled to have a CT scan of his chest, followed by a consultation with the pulmonologist.

When the doctor joined us in the examining room after he had looked over Andy's CT scan results, he gave us some unexpected news.

"It looks like Andy has bronchiectasis," he said.

"Bronchi–*what?*" I asked. *Isn't that some kind of dinosaur?* This was all new terminology to me. "What does that mean?" I asked.

"It means that part of Andy's lung was permanently damaged when he had pneumonia. There are now areas of widened and scarred tissue all throughout his lower left lobe. The secretions in the lung get trapped in these small pockets of flabby lung tissue, and he can't clear his airways unless he coughs." The doctor went on to explain that in normal, healthy lung tissue, the lung secretions get swept through the lung by *cilia:* little hair-like structures that move back and forth, keeping the lung clean. But Andy's cilia in the lower left lobe, along with the rest of the surrounding lung tissue, had been damaged by the Adenovirus infection causing the secretions to get stuck, needing to be coughed up in order to be removed. Unfortunately, once those secretions are coughed up, more mucus is produced and also has to be coughed up. It's a never-ending process.

The doctor did say that children's lungs continue to grow until around age eight or ten; some doctors even think it could be as late as age twelve. He suggested that we might consider having a lobectomy—a surgery which would remove part of Andy's lower left lobe, allowing his body to regenerate new, healthy lung tissue in place of what was removed. If the damage was limited to only a small area of one lobe, surgery may be the best solution.

This frightened me. *Lung surgery?* It sounded to me as though the surgery would have been more beneficial if it had been done earlier, when Andy had more years to grow new lung tissue. For all we knew, Andy probably had bronchiectasis for several years—as long as he had been coughing. Why hadn't the doctors ever looked into this before, instead of saying it was just sinusitis? I wanted to cry.

The pulmonologist told us he would need to consult with the surgeons who actually performed this type of surgery, to see if they thought removing a lobe would help Andy, or instead, be detrimental to him. The pulmonologist also wanted to ask the surgeons if it would be possible to remove only part of a lobe, instead of the whole thing, since the lower left lobe was the largest one in the body. No one wanted to reduce Andy's overall lung capacity if it wouldn't help him in the long run.

"In the meantime, before we even think about surgery, we need to try some other, less invasive procedures," the doctor suggested. "Why don't we try doing some therapy with a compression vest for a month?"

A what?

The doctor left the room for a minute, and when he returned, he was holding a small, black nylon vest with rubber tubes hanging off of it on both sides. "It might help," he said.

What the doctor was suggesting was that we try doing some sort of therapy with the same compression vest commonly used in patients with other obstructive lung conditions, such as Cystic Fibrosis. Andy would strap the vest on, and it would fill up with air and vibrate his chest at different frequencies, shaking him until the mucus was thinned out and loosened up enough to be coughed up more easily. From the minute the doctor first described it, I knew I wanted nothing to do with it. He said the therapy would take about half an hour, and that Andy would need to do it twice a day: once in the morning and once in the evening. While doing therapy with the vest, Andy would also need to use a nebulizer with Albuterol to open up his airways, making the vest more effective.

Another medical procedure added to our daily routine? What am I, a nurse? I can honestly say I was thinking more of my own convenience at the time, rather than Andy's well-being, but I felt like I had already been asked to do enough. I was already giving two-hour-long injections to three boys, once a week. There was also oral medication that needed to be given every day. Now I needed to do lung-shaking therapy on my oldest son twice a day, for half an hour each time? How many hours did these doctors think there were in a day? How were we supposed to fit a half-hour session in before school? Andy already got up at the crack of dawn. I wanted no part of it.

But whether I approved or not, Andy was fitted for a vest before we left the hospital that day. Bart was shown how to use the machine while I sat in the waiting room. The doctor said a new vest and compressor would be shipped to our house for a thirty-day trial period. After that we were to come back to see him, discuss what the surgeons had said, and we would see if the vest had done any good. I was sure that it wouldn't help, but to appease the doctor (as if I had any authority to object to his instructions), I agreed to try it. When it proved useless, which I assumed it would, we would return it to the company that had sent it to us.

From the moment I first hooked Andy up to his vest at home, I was nothing but negative toward this seemingly simple, yet very expensive piece of medical equipment. What was the big deal about this thing, anyway? Each day and night I hooked the vest to Andy, much like buckling up a life jacket. Then I connected two rubber hoses to the vest and then to the machine, plugged it in and turned it on. With the push of a few buttons, it would blow air through the tubes, inflating the vest until it squeezed Andy's chest so hard he could barely breathe, and then he would start shaking. He was supposed to do one half-hour session, comprised of six five-minute intervals, pausing to cough at the end of each one. The pressure and intensity of the vibrations would increase at each interval.

After the thirty days were up, we went back to Minneapolis to see the lung doctor. I wasn't sure if I should pack up the vest and bring it with us to return to the hospital, or if I would simply ship it back to the company that sent it to us. Bart told me just to leave it at home, but I just couldn't wait to get rid of it.

At our appointment, the doctor told us that Andy would not be having lung surgery. The area affected by the bronchiectasis was just too large to remove; the damage wasn't concentrated in one small area, which would have been helpful. Also, the CT scan showed that there was simply too much good lung tissue mixed in with the bad, and the surgery would remove all of this good tissue. Instead of surgery, Andy was to continue on with the vest...indefinitely. After thirty days with the vest, his pulmonary function tests revealed a slight improvement in lung functions, and a repeat chest X-ray showed that the shaded area of his lung looked to be a bit smaller. The vest was the best treatment option available.

NO! Not that horrible thing! I had it all packed up and ready to send back, but now it looked like it was going to be part of our lives for a long time.

18

The Two Columns

I n April 2011, long after the vest had become just another part of our daily routine, I attended a baby shower for our pastor's youngest daughter, who had recently given birth to her first child: a baby girl. A friend of mine, Scotty, was asked to share a short devotional while everyone else snacked on pastel mints and honey roasted peanuts. Scotty headed up to the front of the room holding a pad of paper and a black marker. She drew two columns on the piece of paper. One column had the heading *Me,* while the other read *God.*

While this little exercise was meant for my pastor's daughter, I, along with the other ladies in attendance, listened and watched, trying to apply it personally. Scotty, who was standing up front, explained that we were to mentally place everything we owned (mainly the *big* things) into these two columns, going over each thing one at a time. If we placed the item into the *God* column, then that meant we trusted God with that thing and were willing to let go of it and place it in his hands. If the item ended up in the *Me* column, then we did not trust God with it and would rather take care of it ourselves.

For example: I could put my car into God's column, meaning I trusted God with my car. I was giving it over to him. Whatever he wanted me to do with my car, I would. I wouldn't worry about what would happen to my car, how many miles I was putting on it, or whether or not I parked too close to the car next to me in the parking lot at Target. The car now belonged to God, and it was to be used for his purposes. The same would be true of my house, my marriage, my dog, etc.

As we got further down the list, the items got a little harder to place in God's column because they continued to get more and more important. When we were almost completely through the list, I could still honestly say that so far, everything that had been mentioned could be put into God's column. But then Scotty got to the words *my child*. Obviously, it was no surprise; we were at a baby shower. Scotty just wanted to show in a tangible way that we as mothers need to trust God with our children. But when I thought about it literally—as if I had a column for myself and one for God—I realized that the only things I could *not* put in God's column were my children. Everything else was okay. Trusting God with my children had been a struggle for me since having my very first child, and I never wanted to admit it, even though deep down I always knew it was true.

The issue of trust came up every once in a while, like every time we had our children dedicated, but then I could push it out of my mind again and not deal with it. It wasn't until I was confronted with this issue head-on when Ethan was sick that I even realized that there was a need to trust God with my children. I always thought I could handle them myself. God didn't need to bother with them. They were in good hands: *my* hands. After all, I was the one who stayed up at night with them when they were sick and held them when they were sad. I was the one who called the doctor when Andy had his seizures and when Ethan had a temperature of 105°. These were *my* kids, and I took care of them—and I had learned the hard way that when you give your kids over to the Lord, he just might take them away. I could not trust him. I didn't before, and I *really* didn't now, and I had never really given it much thought until that day at the shower.

Scotty went on to explain that by putting our things in God's column, Satan would have to get through God before he could get at our things. If Satan wanted to destroy my ministry or attack my marriage, if it was under God's care he would have to get through God first. But if Satan wanted to come after anything that was in the *Me* column, he would only need to knock me out of the way first, and then he could have whatever he wanted out of that column. I pictured my kids on one side of me and Satan on the other side, with just me in the middle. I realized that my kids didn't stand a chance with only me to protect them.

Suddenly, I found myself at a crisis point in my faith—yes, another one. I knew I needed to make a decision: trust God or don't. I could almost hear the prelude to my mental highlight film beginning to play as I contemplated my choices.

I didn't know if what was being said in this devotional was actual truth, based on what the Bible said about God in relation to our possessions or our children, or if it was just meant to be figurative—something a new mother could easily remember when learning to trust God with her children. I didn't have time to check the Scriptures and find out for sure. I was at a baby shower, after all.

I did know that I did not have my children in God's column; that was for sure. And by being in my column, I now assumed that Satan was free to do whatever he wanted with them, and I was powerless to stop him. I should have learned of my limitations when Ethan died, but I didn't. I think Ethan's death actually had the opposite effect, and I tried to hold on tighter to my children since God obviously didn't do a good enough job of taking care of Ethan. But after the little shower devotional, I started to wonder, *Did Ethan die because he was in my column and not God's? If I would have trusted God with Ethan earlier, would Ethan still be here?*

I was starting to get tears in my eyes, and I felt like I needed to leave the room immediately, but I also felt like all eyes would be on me for walking out in the middle of the devotional. I didn't want to offend Scotty, who was sharing this devotional. I also didn't want to put a damper on the pastor's daughter's joyous occasion; so I just remained in my seat, red-faced and nervous, willing myself not to cry.

When it was finally over, I took a deep breath, ate my cake and left with a whole new set of questions and no answers. Would this process of asking why, then feeling okay, then asking why again never end? I thought I had come to a good place where I understood that I might never understand, and that was okay. Now I was back to blaming myself for Ethan's death—this time because I hadn't trusted God with my children, and therefore had put Ethan directly in Satan's path, with only myself standing there with my arms clenched tightly around him to protect him. Obviously I did just about as good as could be expected when going up against Satan. If that were truly what had happened, I had failed miserably at protecting my child. I wanted so badly to put the rest of my kids in God's column, but I still didn't know how; I still didn't know how to trust him, or why I should. What if I trusted and lost again? How could I live if it happened…again?

19

Little Boy Lost

At the end of April, only a few weeks after the baby shower, Gavin and Mathew came down with a nasty bout of Rotavirus. I had to drive into town to buy more tasty electrolyte replacement drinks. Since I was going to be in town, Bart had asked me to pick up a few things at the hardware store for a project he was working on. I brought Gavin with me because he was starting to get better, and I knew Bart wouldn't get much work done if he had to watch him.

When Gavin and I returned from the store, I pulled the car into the driveway, let Gavin out of his car seat and headed to the garage to show Bart what I had bought because I wasn't sure if it was what he had wanted. Gavin was digging in his "construction site" in the driveway. I must have been in the garage for a total of five minutes, all the while assuming Gavin was still digging in the driveway. When I went out to check on him he was no longer in his construction site. I asked Bart, "Do you know where Gavin went?"

He looked at me with a questioning look on his face that seemed to ask, "Why don't *you* know where he is?" But all he said was, "No." That was not the answer I was hoping for.

I considered panicking, but thought that I should check all of Gavin's favorite hangouts before doing so. I ran to the back of the house to check the sand box and the swing set—no Gavin. I ran back to the shed where he sometimes liked to sit on the riding lawn mower—no Gavin. I figured he must have gone to the barn in the front yard to sit in Daddy's tractor or grab another shovel or dump truck for his construction site, but when I arrived in the barn there was no sign of him. It was eerily silent outside. I began calling his name, hoping that I would hear his little voice answer back, "What?" like he usually did. But there was no answer. By this time Bart had realized that I had no idea where Gavin was.

"Why did you take him out of his car seat if you weren't ready to watch him?" he asked me.

"Because we were just in the garage, and he was just right here playing in the driveway," I said.

"Well, could he be inside the house?" Bart asked.

"Maybe." We ran inside and called for him. I knew he wasn't very good at opening the door to the house so it was a long-shot, but worth a try. Bart checked upstairs and down—still no sign of him.

By this time I was in an all-out panic. Our house is situated on an eight-acre hayfield surrounded by forty acres of wooded forest and more fields. Beyond the border of our property to the north is heavily wooded state forest land. Adjacent to our property on the south is another thirty-five acre parcel which my parents had bought several years back when they moved to Minnesota. I knew that most likely, Gavin had gone to visit his grandparents. I could just hear him saying, "See Bapa? See Bapa?"

The only problem was that our property and my parents' property are separated by a stream that flows directly into a large river. In April, with the spring thaw running into it, that stream is full to overflowing. My only hope was that Gavin had taken the driveway to get to my parents' house, rather than taking a shortcut through the woods and trying to cross the wobbly, eight-inch-wide board that we used as a bridge across the stream. I ran up the driveway, which is a quarter of a mile long, hoping I'd run into Gavin, knowing full well that the further I ran one way, he could easily be going further away in another direction causing us to get farther and farther apart. But I had to start somewhere. I ran all the way to my parents' house, never running into Gavin, bounded up the front porch steps and knocked on the door.

"Is Gavin here?" I called through the screen door. The bewildered look on my mom's face was all I needed for an answer. She had no idea why Gavin would be there, so I turned and jumped off the front porch, calling behind me, "He's gone. I can't find him." I headed toward their backyard to the stream and the rickety board/bridge. By this time I started praying constantly, "Please, Lord, don't let him be in the stream. Please don't let him be in the stream." I approached the board and hesitantly looked into the stream on either side. I didn't see him, but the water was rushing so fast I wasn't sure, had he fallen in, that he wouldn't have been carried away already. I quickly ran across the board and headed back toward our house, hoping that when I returned Bart would have found Gavin, and the nightmare would be over.

No such luck. "Did you find him?" I asked.

Bart shook his head. He was starting to get impatient. "Where was he when you last saw him?" he asked.

"In the driveway, playing."

"Are you sure?"

"Yes."

"Where did he go after that?" he asked.

"I don't know. I didn't see him go anywhere."

"Just think!"

"I can't! He was in the driveway, and that's all I saw!" We were getting nowhere. I decided to hop in the car since I was completely worn out and out of breath from running. I drove to the road, just in case he had not gone to my parents' house, but instead headed in the other direction toward the road, or worse yet, the river landing. As I drove by the horse pasture, I checked to see if he had crawled under the barbed-wire fence to visit the horses, but I didn't see him. I continued up the driveway, checking the stream and the culvert as I crossed over top, praying that I didn't see anything. By this time my parents had also gotten in their Suburban and were driving the other way, through the hayfield that runs alongside both of our properties.

After I had driven along the road for a bit and had gone down to the river landing and still hadn't found him, a feeling of desperation came over me. I just started calling out to God. I remember shouting, "Lord, help me! Help my little boy! Please help us find him! We don't know where he is, but you do. Please show us where he is! Please keep him safe until we can get to him. Please, Lord!" Over and over I called out to God, begging him to protect Gavin. I didn't feel that I could handle losing another child. I had no idea where he was. I figured we would have found him by now if he was anywhere nearby. He could have wandered into the woods, and we would never be able to find him; it was such a vast area. Where would we even start to look? I wondered if I should call the sheriff and have a search crew come out to the house, but I knew that Gavin hadn't been missing long enough. Even though it seemed like hours to me, it had probably only been about twenty minutes.

It was then, in that moment of desperation and utter helplessness that I finally realized how very small and insignificant I really was. I was one little person with a very limited view. I could only see what was right in front of me. I had no way of knowing where my little boy was. I had one physical body, which was only capable of being in one place at one time. And if that place was not the same place that Gavin was, it didn't do me any good.

In that same moment the truth and reality of God's power and might became ever so real to me. God is omnipresent; he is everywhere all at once. And, he is all-knowing. He knew right where Gavin was, and he could be with him, protecting him while I searched for him. I finally realized that I could trust God, and I had to trust God because I had no other choice! Who was I that I thought I was more capable of caring for my children than their all-powerful, all-loving, all-knowing Creator? How highly did I esteem myself to even think for a moment that I was better than God at keeping them safe?

The image of the two columns kept returning to my mind. Was I still trying to keep my children in my column? Was Gavin in my column even now? A lot of good that would do him since I had no idea where he was! When would I learn my lesson? I had already failed miserably at keeping Ethan and Andy healthy, even though I had done everything in my power to try and do so. (If I didn't learn then about my own limitations, I must be a real hardhead.)

I continued calling out to God until my throat burned and my voice grew hoarse. Again and again I gave Gavin over to the Lord. I told God that Gavin was his child and that I could do nothing to protect him or even find him without God's help.

While Bart continued walking up and down the length of the stream, I pulled the car up to the garage and switched to driving our Suburban so I could also go off-road. I decided to once more drive to the back side of the property where the hay field met up with the woods. When I got to the place where I had to cross the culvert in order to get to the back hay field, I saw my parents' Suburban pulled over to the side. I looked to the left and saw my mom waving her arms and pointing down toward the stream. For a brief moment, I didn't know if I wanted to look; I couldn't tell if the expression on her face was one of relief...or sadness.

When I finally did look, I saw my stepdad coming up from the stream holding Gavin. Gavin was crying, but he was okay. He was reaching his arms out for me. My stepdad called out as loudly as he could, "We found him!" so that if Bart could hear him, he would know he could stop looking. Then we prayed right there on that spot and thanked God for his miraculous protection.

When I looked over at the spot where my parents had found Gavin, I was amazed. It was a place he had never gone before, and it was actually very far away from our house. He had walked quite a distance for such a little boy, especially a boy who had been sick for a week. When my parents found Gavin, he had been sitting right beside the stream, but he was in such a low-lying ditch that I had probably driven right by him and never saw him. Thankfully, my mom had seen him from the other side of the stream and called for my stepdad to go down and get him. I think that maybe Gavin had wanted to go to my parents' house by way of the board/bridge, but when he got to the stream, he was afraid to cross. Instead, he just walked along the stream, hoping to find a place where it would end and he could get around it. Never finding an end to the stream, he must have given up and sat down, frustrated and scared. I was so thankful that Gavin didn't try to cross. He would have been no match for the strong current. I like to think that an angel was sitting next to him while he waited to be found, keeping him safe and calm until we got there.

I learned a valuable lesson about faith that day—one that was very difficult at the time, but so powerful that I will never forget it as long as I live. I realized that up until then, even when I thought I trusted God, it was only because of the things he had done for me. I considered him trustworthy because he guided me to the right college and gave me great friends. He brought a godly man into my life and blessed us with wonderful children. He made things possible when I could see no way on earth that they could ever work out. I guess I believed that God was there to serve me and make things happen for me. I decided whether or not he was trustworthy based upon how well he performed. I would trust him if things worked out the way I wanted them to. I would choose which things I would trust him with and which things I wouldn't—like my children. If bad things ever happened, or things didn't make sense to me, I would take back all of the trust I had placed in him in a heartbeat.

What's true for me is true for anyone else: when we put our trust in God only because of the things he does for us in the good times, our faith is almost sure to flounder during the storms that come into our lives. And believe me, there will be storms. Faith in God needs to be based on something other than the circumstantial; it needs to be based on something rock-solid and unshakable. We need to put our faith in God because he is God—period! He deserves our trust; he doesn't have to earn it. We should trust God because we have no choice *but* to trust him. It sounds so simple, like there must be more, but really, what more does there need to be? God is God and we are not. End of discussion.

20

Enter: Moose

I couldn't end my story without telling about how God finally answered my moose prayer. People often say that when it comes to prayer, God always answers, although he doesn't always say yes. He might say no...or *wait*. I saw my moose prayer as being answered in the negative, but that's not at all what God had in store for me; he had a big surprise. It is nice to think that when God does say no, it's because he has something better for us, even though sometimes we can't think of anything better than what we are asking him for at the time.

I couldn't think of anything better than seeing a moose while on vacation in Glacier National Park. What better way to cap off a wonderful family vacation? I guess I've always tried to control everything in my life. If things would have been done my way, then I would have seen a moose when I thought it would be the best time to see one. Looking back now, I realize that this is just another example of my genie-in-a-bottle approach to God.

One evening in May 2011, Emma and I were driving home after seeing *Beauty and the Beast* performed live at our local performing arts theater. We had just turned onto our driveway when I noticed something about twenty yards away in the hayfield to my left that looked out of place. At first I thought it was one of our horses. "What is Swede doing way out here in Grandpa's field?" I asked Emma.

When we got closer, we saw that it wasn't Swede. Was it one of my stepdad's mules? They had been known to escape from time to time. But further examination of the animal revealed that it was not a mule, or a horse, and it was way too big and dark to be a deer. Its backbone had a funny sort of slope to it, kind of like a…"Moose! Emma, it's a moose!"

I couldn't believe it. I noticed the moose was walking away from me, making a beeline for the road, so I did a U-turn in the driveway and drove in the same direction, parallel to the moose, until I reached the road. I turned right onto the road and drove straight toward her, arriving just in time for her to walk right in front of my car, about ten feet from me, on her way to the woods on the other side of the road. I was thankful that Emma was there to back me up when I told my story because I did not have my camera with me. There are not many moose sightings in our area, and I was afraid no one would believe me!

To think, I had wanted to see a moose out in Montana and was disappointed with God for not delivering, when all the time he was probably saying, "Just wait." He had even better plans: a moose by my own driveway! Right here where I live! God did answer my prayer. Yes, it was four years later, but it was even more than I could have asked for. Being surprised was so much better. (Next time, I will pray more specifically to see a bull moose. Antlers would have been much more impressive.) But for now, I'm satisfied. Beggars can't be choosers…can they?

21

Lessons Learned

The past five years since Ethan's death have put some distance between me and the tragedy itself, which has allowed me to gain a little perspective on all of the things God has taught me through the experience of losing a child. I often say that I have learned so much from losing Ethan; I only wish that the lessons could have come an easier way. Unfortunately, that doesn't seem to be the way life works. I hope that what God has taught me through my trials could in some way be helpful for someone else out there who may be just starting out in the grief process.

No one said life would be easy. Sometimes I think that as Christians, we get this idea in our heads that we are somehow above suffering—as if becoming part of God's family makes us immune to the problems of this world. This simply isn't true.

In the early days following Ethan's death, while researching the Bible for my monthly church newsletter articles, I came across numerous verses that compared life to a race. Many times in these verses the biblical authors exhorted their audience to persevere, to endure, to finish the race. Before losing Ethan, I could never completely relate to these verses. Why all this talk about life being hard? Why compare life to a race? Races are no fun. Running is strenuous. Why not compare life to a picnic next to a waterfall on a warm summer day? That's how I viewed life—up until Ethan died; everything was all well and good. There were small obstacles, yes, but they could easily be overcome with time. I had so much to look forward to, like material gains, wedded bliss, and giving birth to beautiful babies!

However, after our tragedy, life became almost unbearable. Material possessions didn't matter and certainly brought no pleasure. There was no longer anything to look forward to except possibly more sickness or even death. Suddenly these race metaphors began to make sense to me. I don't know about you, but any time I've ever run in a race (which has only happened once), it wasn't exactly relaxing, or even enjoyable; it was hard work (which is why it has only happened once). By the end of the race, I was overjoyed to see the finish line in front of me and just couldn't wait to be done.

2 Timothy 4:8 says, "I have fought the good fight, I have finished the race, I have kept the faith. Now there is in store for me the crown of righteousness, which the Lord, the righteous Judge, will award to me on that day—and not only to me, but also to all who have longed for his appearing." God has promised us eternal life if we believe in his Son, and in eternity there will be no more suffering or sadness. No more pain. We have to believe that the joy that awaits us in heaven is incomparable to the suffering that we may experience now.

Romans 8:18 promises this: "For I consider that the sufferings of this present time are not worthy to be compared with the glory which shall be revealed in us." All I can say is: yes, life can be hard, especially when you face the loss of a beloved child. The only thing we can do is keep going, with the help of our Lord Jesus Christ, and look forward to seeing our loved ones in heaven someday, where we will never again be separated.

Some things may never make sense. As I said earlier, I had been plagued by the question *why* ever since losing my son. After a while I would just chalk it up to God's will and that would satisfy me, but only for a time. Then the questions would return. I began to wonder if there would ever be an answer that would satisfy my longing to know the truth. If I had the opportunity to sit face-to-face with God and ask him why he allowed Ethan to die at such a young age, would there be anything God could say that would make me feel okay with everything? Would there really be an answer that would make me say, "Oh, well then in *that* case, I'm fine with it. That makes total sense to me. I would have done the same thing." I doubt it. What if I asked God why Ethan had to die, and God told me that Ethan's life and death would have caused three people to come to a saving knowledge of Jesus Christ; that it was just the thing that would cause them to really think about what was important in life, and if Ethan hadn't died, those three people would go to hell. Would that be a good enough reason to justify my going through this grief? Would it be okay with me then? Probably not. Instead I would probably ask, "Couldn't you have picked someone else's baby?"

In Isaiah 55:8–9, the Bible says this: "'For my thoughts are not your thoughts, neither are your ways my ways,' declares the Lord. 'As the heavens are higher than the earth, so are my ways higher than your ways and my thoughts than your thoughts.'" To me that means that God has his reasons, and we may never understand them. Whether or not I ever find out what those reasons are in reference to my personal situation, it wouldn't change a thing. I am still here, and Ethan is not. And until I am in heaven with him, there will always be that huge, gaping hole in my life. Knowing why that hole is there would not remove the pain of it. Sometimes I think that not knowing *why* might even be better, in case I don't like the answer. Although I can't seem to stop myself from wondering *why* from time to time, I have to realize that asking is futile.

I am not the first, nor will I be the last mother to lose a child. Shortly after Ethan passed away, I tried to get my hands on every book about losing a child that I could. Believe me, there aren't many, especially if you eliminate the books that try to tell you that your child could actually still be living in your house…as a ghost—then you're really limited. I found little comfort in the books I did read because I couldn't relate to the situations presented in them—they were just too different from mine. One book was about a mother who had suffered several miscarriages and had two stillborn sons. I thought to myself, *My situation is worse. My child was alive for nine months! I was really attached to him.*

If the book was about an adult child who was lost, I would think, *Well at least he or she got to live for thirty-some years. You got more time than I did; my kid never even got to say his first word! My situation is still worse!* I could not relate to any of these other people's stories because in my mind, they didn't even come close to being as bad as mine. To me, what I went through was the worst thing that any person had ever experienced or ever would in the history of human existence!

Now after several years, I know that that just isn't true; it only seemed that way because it was happening to *me.* As strange as it may sound, I think I was actually taking pride in my grief and how painful it was to lose Ethan. Maybe if I had the saddest story ever told, I would in some way *win.* What I would win, I don't know, but it was better than losing. I had already lost enough.

The year after Ethan died we took a little trip to the North Dakota farm country where my husband's grandparents had homesteaded. We wanted to see the cemetery where my husband's uncle, who died when he was only a few days old, was buried. As I walked around this old Finnish cemetery, I was struck by the number of gravestones that belonged to children. Even more sobering were the rows of gravestones belonging to entire families. There were mothers, fathers and children whose deaths had all occurred within days of each other. I figured that these families must have contracted some sort of contagious disease, and it simply wiped them out.

I began to realize that it wasn't that long ago that the death of a child, especially an infant, was a pretty common occurrence. Although most of the gravestones in that North Dakota cemetery had been put there in the late 1800s, some of them were from the 1930s and 40s. When you think about how long humans have been on this planet, that's really not that long ago. It is only in recent times that the death of a child has become more of a rarity, due in large part to modern-day medical care.

Even today in countries around the world, there are entire families of children wiped out from malnutrition, and waterborne or mosquito-borne illnesses that could be prevented if only there were better medical care, more financial aid, or prevention education available.

Realizing this has actually caused me to feel a sort of kinship with the mothers of these children. I know that we share a bond born of experience, and we would understand each other like no one else could, even though we may live in very different times or places. As my one friend, who lost her three-year-old daughter to cancer said to me after Ethan died: "You are now part of *The Club*. It's an exclusive club, and none of the members ever asked to join, nor do they actually want to be in this club—yet here we all are."

So know this: If you belong to the *Grieving Parents Club,* you are not the only member.

God can bring good out of my situation, but it won't ease the pain. For years after Ethan's death I struggled with Romans 8:28 and God's promise to make "...all things work together for good to those who love God." For a while I was confused and believed that God had caused Ethan's death to bring about a certain good—as if his death were actually a means to an end. Now I understand that rather than causing Ethan's death to bring about a certain good, God has actually promised only to make things work together for good *after* Ethan's death. Now that it has happened, God is not going to let any of our tears or struggles go to waste. He will use them, and he will bring good out of the rubble of our lives. This will not change the fact that we are sad and that we miss our son very much.

One good thing that God has brought about is the opportunity for me to share my story with others. It actually feels pretty gratifying to be used by God to reach those who could only be reached by someone who has been there herself. It makes it seem like everything I went through was not in vain.

Don't I wish that instead, God had asked me to become wealthy so that I could better minister to those who must bear the burden of having way too much money? Sometimes. I think this is a lot harder, but this is where I find myself, and so this is where I will serve: along this dark road that has only been traveled by a few, and can only be understood by someone who has walked the path herself.

God understands. Several months before Ethan passed away, God had lined up a little ministry for me, writing monthly articles for our church's newsletter. At first it was an avenue for me to use my passion for writing in a way that would honor God. It also gave my pastor, who had been writing the articles himself, a little more free time. At first I viewed these articles more like a school assignment. I would have to think of a topic, look up a bunch of verses, and do some research. But by the time the April newsletter article came out on April 2, 2006, my assignments had changed.

I had written that April article from the computer in the waiting room down the hall from Ethan and Andy's hospital room and e-mailed it to my church. Ethan passed away very early the next morning, less than twenty-four hours after the people in my church got their newsletters. Then it seemed that I had been placed in the perfect position to share with my congregation what God was teaching me while I was going through the loss of my son.

That April article was an Easter article, and I wrote about how God understood exactly what I was going through, watching my two sons suffer in the hospital. God, too, had to stand by as his only Son suffered and died on the cross. Just as I could do nothing to stop Ethan from dying, God couldn't stop Jesus from dying on the cross. (Actually, he could have, but that would have ruined everything.) He had to allow it to happen so that we could all have the opportunity to spend eternity in heaven with him. I'm sure it was painful for the Father to stand by and allow Jesus to suffer on the cross, instead of jumping in and simply putting an end to it.

In much the same way, it was painful for me to sit helplessly and watch Andy and Ethan lying unconscious in their hospital beds with breathing tubes taped to their mouths, wondering whether or not they would survive. But there was one big difference between my situation and God's: God was allowing his Son to suffer on purpose...for us. If Jesus didn't die on the cross, none of us would stand a chance of going to heaven. Our sin would always stand in the way of having that right relationship with God. Only the spotless Lamb Jesus was a qualified substitute for the punishment we deserved: death.

I, on the other hand, did not choose to let my children suffer. If I had been given the option, I would have chosen not to—even if it were the only way to save someone else. I'm just not that strong and not that loving, I guess. But God is. And whenever I think that no one can understand what I am going through; whenever I think about Ethan and how much I miss him, and wonder why all of this ever had to happen, I can look at the cross and I am instantly reminded that God understands, and he cares. He cared enough to send his Son, and now that I know how painful that can be, it means a whole lot more.

I did not fail my child. After the loss of a child, it is only natural to ask the question, "Why do bad things happen to good people?" Of course, one would probably be asking this question in a rhetorical sense, since many different answers exist, and some of them are way out in left field and seem very contrary to what the Bible says about God. Unfortunately, from time to time, someone may feel the need to answer this question for you, whether you wanted an answer or not.

One of those explanations that I heard several times after Ethan died is that if I would have only had more faith, God would have healed Ethan. Therefore, it was my fault that Ethan died, due to my lack of faith. Well that was comforting, considering I had just lost my child and was already struggling with blaming myself for his death. Why not hit me again while I'm down?

I actually believed this lie for quite a while until one day at a Bible study, I realized something that, for some reason, I had never realized before. Yes, Ethan did die, even though many people were praying for him, including me. But he wasn't the only one in the hospital at the time; I had two sons who were struggling to survive the same disease. For a while, it had seemed that Andy was even sicker than Ethan was. Both boys were being prayed for by the same people, with the same amount of faith, and only Ethan died. Andy survived. How could it have been because of my lack of faith? If that were the case, both boys would be gone.

For some reason, God, in his sovereignty, chose to allow Ethan to die and not Andy. As I said, I may never understand that, and I now realize that I really don't need to know why. But I do know this: it is not helpful at all to tell someone who has just lost a loved one that if he or she would have had more faith, then that loved one may have survived. Comments like that only further wound the brokenhearted and do more harm than good.

First and foremost we must remember that God is sovereign. He is in control, even when it seems like we could have made a better choice when it comes to how the universe is run. We must remember that this world is under the curse of sin, and until Jesus returns, defeats Satan, puts an end to sin for good, and God creates a new heaven and a new Earth, he is going to have to work with what he has: a sin-cursed world. In this world, people get sick and die. Terrible accidents happen. God never said they wouldn't. Our hope doesn't lie in this world; it lies in the next and in the One who is preparing that place for us even now.

Worrying about our children does not protect them. As I have already made very clear, I have been a worrier all my life. My grandma is the same way, so it must be genetic—just one more thing in my life with a genetic root. When it came to my children, I worried about a wide scope of things: diseases, car accidents, anything that could take them from me. I figured that by worrying, I was actually preparing myself for the inevitable. That way, when it did happen, I would somehow know what to do. Maybe I would even be able to prevent it from happening by worrying about it ahead of time. This was just another example of me thinking I had superhuman child-protection abilities.

In the end, I spent an awful lot of time worrying about things that never happened, and the one thing that *did* happen came out of nowhere, took me completely by surprise, and there was nothing I could do to stop it. Maybe if I had worried about the children having an immune deficiency, then Ethan would still be here, right? Of course not!

In Matthew 6:27 Jesus asks, "Who of you by worrying can add a single hour to his life?" (Or his child's life for that matter?) I worried plenty about Ethan, and it certainly didn't help him at all. I only cast a shadow on the small amount of time I did have with him by spending so much of it worrying about things that never happened. When he was born on the Fourth of July, I worried about how we would spend his birthday every year, since we would most likely be at a parade followed by a family picnic, leaving no time for a birthday party. Well, he never even made it to his first birthday, so all of the hours spent worrying about what we would do every July Fourth were a complete waste of my time. Looking back now, I would give anything to still have to deal with the problem of when to celebrate Ethan's birthday!

*A **little perspective goes a long way.*** When Andy first started "doing his vest," as we say, I'll admit I had a bit of an attitude problem toward it. I viewed it as an inconvenience, since Andy had to sit on the couch for half an hour, twice a day, with nothing to do but read or watch television. When we first got the vest, it was late winter and I had gotten hooked on watching my favorite musical talent competition on television, as I did every year. It was time for the show's annual fundraising episode, in which the contestants and judges traveled to different parts of the world, raising money and awareness for different issues such as poverty or malaria.

One of the hosts of the show traveled somewhere in the southern United States to give one very special young girl a gift that would change her life and improve her health: the Vest Airway Clearance System. This young girl had a serious lung disease called Primary Ciliary Dyskinesia, and up until she was given the vest, she had trouble breathing, and her parents had to travel to a far-away clinic so she could receive her treatments. The costs were beginning to add up, but once she had her own vest, she could stay at home and stay healthier.

I remember how grateful her parents were when the host of the show opened the door to their home, and a man came in behind him carrying the vest in its custom-made duffel bag. There were tears in their eyes, and they could not express how thankful they were for such a gift. (The vest is not cheap.) And here I was viewing the vest as a curse—just *one more thing* that I had to do for my child, when actually, it was a gift. Who knows what further damage would have been done to Andy's lungs if he hadn't begun treatment with the vest? I felt so ashamed of my selfish behavior. I thanked God for the new perspective I had gained from the television show and asked him to forgive me for my negative attitude. I prayed that he would give me the grace to continue caring for my children, no matter what little "extras" were required of me. Sometimes it just helps to walk a mile—even a virtual mile—in someone else's shoes before you can really appreciate the path you've been asked to walk.

Conclusion

The lessons that I learned about trust the day Gavin got lost have not answered all of my questions. Even now, when I think about Ethan and how old he would be, or what he would be doing if he were still on earth, the old questions *why* and *what if* come creeping back to my mind. There is still so much I do not understand.

The one thing that has changed is this: whenever I am faced with a situation in which I need to trust God, my mind no longer plays for me the same old highlight film of my life's greatest disappointments. It's as if the default settings in my brain have been changed. Now I simply remember what God taught me on the day that Gavin got lost and I know, without a doubt, that there is no use putting all my hope and trust in myself. And although I am still tempted at times to take back control of the reigns when it comes to my kids, all I have to do is review my new mental video footage—the image of Gavin sitting alone by the stream, with God's arms around him—and I am reminded of my smallness, my limitations, my own humanity. Then I give my children back over to the Lord…again.

I will never have all the answers. I cannot give anyone else the answers they seek when they experience terrible loss. Some things only the Lord knows. One thing I will do is continue to trust him. What other choice do I have? God is and will continue to be faithful. He is the only one I know who is all-powerful, ever-present, all-knowing and all-loving. I would challenge you to find anyone with better qualifications in whom you should place your trust.

Trust in the Lord with all your heart and lean not on your own understanding; in all your ways acknowledge him, and he will make your paths straight.
—Proverbs 3:5–6

About the Author

Jessica Leigh Johnson is a stay-at-home mom who spends most of her time taking care of Emma, Andy, Mathew and Gavin. She volunteers at her children's school once a week, and is actively involved in various children's ministries at her church. She is passionate about music ministry and offering comfort and hope to those who are grieving.

Jessica graduated from Crown College in 1999 with a BS in Christian Education. She and her husband, Bart, live in northern Minnesota.

Notes

All Scripture quotations, unless otherwise indicated, are taken from the *Holy Bible, New International Version*®. *NIV*®. Copyright © 1973, 1978, 1984 by International Bible Society. Used by permission of Zondervan. All rights reserved.

Chapter 4: Everywhere, Red Flags
1. Gertrude Crampton, *Tootle* (New York: Golden Books Publishing, Inc., 1945, 1973).

Chapter 9: The "Aha" Moment
2. The Immune Deficiency Foundation, *Patient and Family Handbook for Primary Immune Deficiency Diseases,* 3rd ed. (Baltimore: 2001), 12.

Chapter 12: The New Normal
3. Ecclesiastes 1:2.

Chapter 13: Denial, I Didn't Recognize You!
4. 1 Thessalonians 4:13–18.

Resources

American Lung Association
(800) 586-4872
www.lung.org

CaringBridge
1715 Yankee Doodle Road
Suite 301
Eagan, MN 55121
(651) 452-7940
www.caringbridge.org

The Compassionate Friends
P.O. Box 3696
Oak Brooke, IL 60522-3696
(630) 990-0010

The Immune Deficiency Foundation
40 West Chesapeake Ave
Suite 308
Towson, MD 21204
(800) 296-4433
www.primaryimmune.org

The Jeffrey Modell Foundation
A non-profit research foundation devoted to primary immune deficiency diseases.

780 Third Ave
New York, NY 10017
(212) 819-0020
(800) JEFF-844
(866) INFO-4-PI
www.jmfworld.org

Ronald McDonald House Charities
One Kroc Drive
Oak Brooke, IL 60523
(630) 623-7048
www.rmhc.org

Smile Again Ministries
P.O. Box 563
Crosslake, MN 56442
(320) 310-8877
www.smileagainministries.com